SOCIAL SECURITY

SOCIAL SECURITY

Prospects for Real Reform

edited by Peter J. Ferrara

CATO
INSTITUTE

Library of Congress Cataloging in Publication Data
Main entry under title:

Social security.

    Includes bibliographical references.
    1. Social security—United States.   I. Ferrara,
Peter J., 1956–   II. Title.

HD7125.S5993   1985   368.4'3'00973   85-9642
ISBN 0-932790-45-3
ISBN 0-932790-48-8 (pbk.)

Printed in the United States of America.

CATO INSTITUTE
224 Second Street SE
Washington, D.C. 20003

For my mother

Contents

Introduction

Early in 1982, Rep. J. J. Pickle (D-Tex.), chairman of the House Subcommittee on Social Security, visited a high school in his district. During a question and answer session, as reported in the *Washington Post*, one student shocked him with a question he never thought he'd hear. "Will social security be around when we get it?"

"Yes, very definitely," the congressman responded. He turned the question around, asking how many of the students expected social security to exist when they retired. Nearly half the students indicated they did not expect the program to exist, telling their congressman in effect that they did not believe him.[1]

This was no isolated reaction. A *Washington Post*–ABC News poll in early 1982 found that 66 percent of those under 45, and 74 percent of those under 30, believe that the program will not even be in existence when they retire.[2] A 1981 *New York Times*–CBS poll found that 73 percent of all Americans had "little or no confidence" in social security's ability to provide retirement benefits for them or their spouses.[3]

This skepticism is well founded, but the public generally does not yet know the half of it. While all the attention has been focused on the financing problems of the program, a new and potentially even more destabilizing problem has been developing. The rate of return paid by social security on the tax funds paid into the system has been falling steadily. Today's retirees are still receiving a good deal from the program in return for past tax payments. But for those entering the work force today, *even if they receive all the social security benefits they are currently promised,* the program will still be a miserable deal, given the enormous tax burden to be imposed under current law over their working careers.

As demonstrated in chapter 1, for many of these workers, social

---

[1]Dan Balz, "Public Increasingly Doubts Survival of Social Security," *Washington Post*, p. A1.

[2]Ibid.

[3]Ibid.

1

security now promises no more than a zero or even negative real rate of return. For the great majority, the program promises returns sharply below readily available market returns on capital investment. If these workers could invest the same amounts as paid into social security in private IRA-type vehicles, they could receive much higher benefits. This is the emerging, new, blockbuster problem for social security. As this problem becomes more widely understood, the social security status quo will become politically untenable.

This is a problem, moreover, that clearly cannot be solved within the current structure of social security. The tax burden on today's young workers cannot be reduced because the revenues are needed to finance benefits for today's elderly. Yet, future benefits for today's young workers cannot be raised because it will be difficult even to pay currently promised benefits. This problem can be solved only through real, fundamental reform, breaking out of the anachronistic structure of the current system.

Social security still faces serious financial problems, particularly over the long term, that make the payment of even the inadequate returns currently promised to today's young workers highly questionable at best. Under the Social Security Administration's (SSA) own so-called pessimistic set of assumptions, paying all the benefits promised to those entering the work force today would require total payroll tax rates of 37.5 percent,[4] an absurd tax burden that will never be accepted by America's workers. The SSA itself in effect admits that this development is at least possible. Many outside observers believe that these projections are in fact the most realistic,[5] and surely they are the most prudent. Reality could reasonably turn out worse.

The program's troublesome long-term financial outlook is due to the fundamental nature of the program. Social security operates on a pay-as-you-go basis, with the tax funds paid into the system today

---

[4]*1985 Annual Report of the Board of Trustees of the Federal Old-Age and Survivors Insurance and Disability Insurance Trust Funds* (Washington: Government Printing Office, March 28, 1985). (Hereafter this will be cited as: *1985 OASDI Report.*) See discussion below, in chapter 2.

[5]See, e.g., Rita Ricardo-Campbell, "Social Security Reform: A Mature System in an Aging Society," in *To Promote Prosperity: U.S. Domestic Policy in the Mid-1980s*, ed. John H. Moore (Stanford: Hoover Institution, 1984); Peter J. Ferrara, *Social Security: The Inherent Contradiction* (Washington: Cato Institute, 1980), chap. 5; and idem, *Social Security: Averting the Crisis* (Washington: Cato Institute, 1982), chap. 5.

not saved for the future benefits of today's workers, but immediately paid out to finance the benefits of today's beneficiaries. This financial structure leaves the program vulnerable to swings in any of a number of unstable economic, social, and demographic factors. And a true demographic disaster has shaped up for social security over the long term. The large baby-boom generation born soon after World War II would naturally put an excessive strain on a pay-as-you-go system when it retires. But to make matters worse, the baby boom was immediately succeeded by a baby bust, with especially low fertility following the baby boom for 25 years now. This means there will be an especially small number of workers to finance benefits for the huge baby-boom generation when it retires, requiring especially high tax rates.

But the worst could be yet to come. All it would take to turn this disastrous situation into an apocalyptic one is the development over the next 30 to 40 years of expensive medical technology effective in substantially lengthening life expectancies. The accounting profession knows no ledgers sufficient to account for the long-term financial outlook of social security if baby boomers were to live 10 years or so longer than now projected, along with higher medical costs. Yet, with our rapidly developing modern technology and today's healthier lifestyles, is this possibility so remote?

The combination of the large baby-boom generation currently swelling the labor force plus further scheduled tax increases helps the financial prospects of social security over the short run. But the system is not immune from a further collapse even over this period. The deficits of the Hospital Insurance portion of the program (HI) would themselves eventually absorb most of the surpluses projected to start in the 1990s for the rest of social security (OASDI).[6] This, along with economic performance similar to that during the 1970s, would be enough for the program to collapse again near the end of the next decade, just when it is supposed to be accumulating large surpluses to aid in the payment of benefits to the baby boomers.

The SSA's own projections again show this. Under the supposedly pessimistic Alternative III assumptions, which assume better

---

[6]Social security is composed of Old-Age and Survivors Insurance (known as OASI), Disability Insurance (known as DI), and Hospital Insurance (known as HI). OASI plus DI is known as OASDI. OASDI plus HI, constituting the entire program, is known as OASDHI.

3

economic performance than in the 1970s, the latest projections show that absorbing the HI deficits into the rest of the program leaves social security unable to pay promised benefits again by the late 1990s.[7]

The short-term prospects for social security are brightened by the current economic rebound. But if the warnings about the economic effect of today's large budget deficits are right, then social security can be expected to collapse again soon. Indeed, if the late-1984 economic downturn had turned into a full-scale recession, the program would now be facing another collapse in the short term. The program is still not immune from financial collapse due to the ravages of periodic recession.

The recurring financial crises of the program are, of course, most harmful to the elderly. They are left as pawns in a political game, frightened over possible political deadlock or inaction, suffering periodic benefit cuts that are irreplaceable at this late date. Our parents and grandparents deserve better.

The elderly are completely at the mercy of political whim, for the Supreme Court held in 1960 that social security beneficiaries have no legally enforceable, contractual entitlement to their benefits and that the government can reduce or cut off such benefits completely at any time. The Court said in *Flemming* v. *Nestor:* "To engraft upon the social security system a concept of 'accrued property rights' would deprive it of the flexibility and boldness in adjustment to everchanging conditions which it demands."[8] Justice Black described the meaning of this decision in his dissent:

> The Court consoles those whose insurance is taken away today, and others who may suffer the same in the future, by saying that a decision requiring the Social Security system to keep faith would deprive it of . . . flexibility and boldness. . . . People who pay premiums for insurance usually think they are paying for insurance, not for flexibility and boldness.[9]

There are other deeply troubling problems with the social security status quo. The program's payroll tax is an enormously regressive element in our tax structure, shifting the federal tax burden substantially toward labor and toward low- and moderate-income workers in particular. Already, for more than half of all workers

[7] *1985 OASDI Report*, app. E.
[8] 363 U.S. 610 (1960), p. 616.
[9] Ibid., p. 624.

4

covered by social security today, the combined employer-employee payroll tax is more than they pay in federal income tax.[10] In 1984, payroll tax revenues, drawn primarily from low- and moderate-income workers, were 80 percent greater than total federal corporate and business tax revenues.[11] A married worker with two children and earning $7,400 in 1985 would pay about $520 in payroll taxes, with another $520 from his employer that probably comes out of his wages as well, before having to pay a dime in federal income tax. Liberals should ask themselves whether these payroll taxes go to pay benefits to recipients who are in greater need than this worker.

As discussed in chapter 4, the payroll tax also serves as a major drag on employment, particularly for lower-income workers. The program also probably does cause a large loss of savings, resulting in substantially slower economic growth.

Social security's benefit structure is also highly inequitable. Two workers paying the same taxes over their working careers may receive widely differing benefit amounts. These inequities bear particularly harshly on single workers, childless workers and two-earner couples. The program, as a result, is especially poorly suited to many working women. Social security essentially still says to women today: get married, stay home, and have lots of children.[12]

Blacks and other minorities with lower life expectancies than the rest of the population also suffer from serious inequities. These groups face the same tax rates as everyone else during their working years, but tend to live fewer years in retirement to collect benefits. A black male at birth today can expect to live 64.8 years, more than 2 years less than necessary for him to qualify for full social security retirement benefits. This black male could actuarially expect only 50 percent of the retirement benefits of a white male because of his lower life expectancy. In addition, blacks as a group are much younger than the rest of the population. Since the program is a worse deal the younger one is, it hurts blacks especially due to this factor as well.

[10]Benjamin Bridges, Jr., "Family Social Security Taxes Compared with Federal Income Taxes, 1979," *Social Security Bulletin* (December 1981).

[11]Council of Economic Advisers, *1985 Economic Report of the President* (Washington: Government Printing Office, 1985).

[12]For more detailed discussion of these inequities, see Ferrara, *The Inherent Contradiction*, chap. 6.

Social security's sheer size is also a major problem. The program, including Medicare, accounts for almost 30 percent of total federal spending. Add in national defense and net interest on the national debt, and the total climbs to over 70 percent. Conservatives need to recognize that any substantial reduction in the size and scope of government is quite unlikely unless something is done about social security. Liberals, on the other hand, must recognize that the public has a tolerance limit for Big Government and that the ever-expanding, elephantine social security system is in effect crowding out other programs targeted to the poor.

Conservatives should also be especially concerned that social security makes the entire elderly population substantially dependent on the government. It is indeed a truly radical departure from a private market economy to require all Americans to rely on the government for the bulk of their income for a major portion of their lives.

All this definitely does not mean that the elderly must be sacrificed in some way to solve the problems of social security. Quite the contrary, fundamental social security reform must benefit the elderly as well as others. For there will frankly be no real, fundamental reform that does not have widespread approval from the retired generation.

Fortunately, fundamental reform can be structured to address the problems of social security without benefit cuts for the elderly or tax increases for workers. Such reform would involve the creation of "Super IRAs," an expanded version of currently available Individual Retirement Accounts. Workers would have the freedom to choose to substitute Super IRAs for some, and eventually all, of their social security coverage through a carefully structured option designed at the same time to maintain, and indeed strengthen, essential social security financing.

A detailed proposal for such reform is presented in chapter 11. This proposal is structured in every way possible to be attractive and beneficial to the elderly today, as well as to today's workers and tomorrow's elderly. The proposal is based on a firm and final rejection of the notion of cutting social security benefits as a means of solving the problems of the program.

Doesn't it make simple sense to act now and avoid the potential economic and social disaster of the baby-boom generation retiring under the current system? Through the proposed Super-IRA reform, baby boomers could be relying heavily on their own individual savings pools in retirement and less heavily on social security. They would be allowed to receive market returns on these funds through the Super IRAs, and much higher benefits, instead of the scandalous returns and inadequate benefits offered them by social security. The additional savings through the Super IRAs could allow today's workers a greater opportunity to work in a more healthy and growing economy now. The benefits paid through the Super IRAs would be entirely equitable, with each worker receiving back what he paid in, plus interest, on an actuarial basis.

Unfortunately, the views of political leaders regarding social security have been dominated by a rigid establishment old guard, which refuses to acknowledge any serious problems in the program, and will consider only marginal, tinkering tax-and-benefit changes. The attitudes of the old guard regarding social security can be summed up in the motto of the three monkeys: hear no evil, see no evil, speak no evil. Every few years, the old guard comes together, agrees to a round of tax increases and benefit cuts to save the system from bankruptcy, and announces to the world that the system will be financially sound well into the next century, citing each other as authorities for the point.

As financing problems for social security develop, the old guard simply favors relying on increased taxes as much as possible for the solution. The possibility of payroll tax rates of 33 percent or more does not alarm the old guard; they simply view such taxes as the price for civilization. The official position of the old guard, believe it or not, is that workers will be able to afford these taxes if they just have fewer children.

This outdated old guard does not in fact represent the views of the broad majority of Americans. Not only do the young doubt the future of the program and the elderly fear the present, but the elderly themselves are deeply concerned about the legacy they will leave for their children and grandchildren. Real, fundamental reform guaranteeing the elderly their expected benefits while offering today's workers a true opportunity for a secure and prosperous retirement in their future would directly address all these concerns. It can consequently be a broadly popular issue, as we shall see in more detail.

This book focuses on such real, fundamental reform and its prospects. Most of the papers published in this volume were first presented at a conference on social security reform held by the Cato Institute in Washington, D.C., in June 1983, and published in the *Cato Journal* 3, no. 2, (Fall 1983). The editor has added commentary on these papers, plus four additional papers addressing key issues. The individual authors are in no way responsible for the commentary provided by the editor. Similarly, the editor does not endorse all the statements made by each of the authors.

The first section deals with the current state of social security. Chapter 1 comprises a paper by the editor and John R. Lott, assistant professor of economics at Texas A&M University, presenting a detailed analysis of the rates of return promised by social security to those entering the work force today. Chapters 2 and 3 discuss the financial foundation of social security in papers by A. Haeworth Robertson, former chief actuary of the Social Security Administration, and Paul Craig Roberts, former assistant secretary for economic policy in the U.S. Treasury and now William E. Simon Professor of Political Economy at Georgetown University. Chapter 4 addresses social security's impact on the national economy with a paper by former treasury undersecretary for economic policy Norman B. Ture. In Chapter 5, the editor examines the reasons for social security's original political acceptance and past popularity, and why its political foundation is now entering a phase of deep erosion.

The second section is made up of papers offering valuable insights into the possibilities for real, fundamental reform. In chapter 6, John C. Goodman, associate professor of economics at the University of Dallas, examines the experiences of Great Britain and Chile, which have implemented reform granting workers the option of substituting private sector alternatives for national social security systems. In chapter 7, Carolyn L. Weaver, associate professor of economics at Virginia Polytechnic and State University, contributes key original historical work concerning the politics of the adoption of social security in the 1930s. In chapter 8, David Ranson, general partner and senior economist at H.C. Wainwright & Co., provides a framework of policy criteria for evaluating fundamental social security reform proposals. Two economists from the Heritage Foundation, Stuart Butler and Peter Germanis, combine in chapter 9 to offer strategic analysis concerning the design of politically feasible fundamental reform. The editor then addresses in chapter 10 some theoretical implications of shifting from a public pay-as-you-go system, like social security, to a private fully funded system.

In the final section, the editor presents a detailed reform proposal for the adoption of Super IRAs, showing why such a proposal is both economically and politically feasible.

THE STATE OF SOCIAL SECURITY

I. Rates of Return Promised by Social Security to Today's Young Workers

Peter J. Ferrara and John R. Lott, Jr.

Those who retired in the early years of social security received high, above-market returns through the program on the limited social security taxes they paid during their working years. Although today's retirees are receiving less of a good deal, they are still enjoying above-market returns. But those now entering the work force will receive unacceptably low, below-market returns, negative in many cases, even in the unlikely event that they receive all the program's currently promised benefits.[1]

In this chapter we will discuss why this pattern of returns is an inevitable result of social security's fundamental method of operation. We will then present empirical calculations indicating that the program does, in fact, offer today's young workers low, below-market returns.

Early Retirees and the Start-Up Phase of a Pay-As-You-Go System

Social security is said to operate on a "pay-as-you-go" basis. That is, the taxes paid into the system by today's workers are not saved to pay for those workers' benefits, as in a fully funded system, but instead are immediately paid out to finance the benefits of current beneficiaries. Similarly, the benefits of today's workers are to be paid out of the taxes of the next generation of workers.

When a pay-as-you-go system is begun, the first generation of workers immediately begins to pay taxes into the system. But there are no accumulated benefit obligations, since the first generation of retirees paid nothing into the system during their working years, when the system was not yet in existence. Nevertheless, because

---

John R. Lott, Jr., is visiting assistant professor of economics at Texas A&M University.

[1]See discussion in chapter 2.

taxes paid into the new system are not saved and invested, they can be used to pay full benefits to those in or near retirement at the time. These full benefits naturally represent very high returns on whatever relatively little amount of taxes these workers may have paid in their last few working years before retirement.

Over the years, however, the returns paid by the pay-as-you-go system will fall steadily, as workers retire who have paid the program's taxes for more and more of their working years. Once workers start retiring who have paid full social security taxes for their entire careers, the system's return reaches a steady state that can continue stably into the future. The period after this point can be labeled the "mature phase" of a pay-as-you-go system; the period before it, the "start-up" phase. As our analysis suggests, it takes at least a generation to pass from the start-up phase to the mature phase.

This analysis explains the high returns previously experienced by social security recipients. Those who retired soon after the program was adopted in the 1930s received quite high returns because they paid the program's taxes for only a few years before retirement and yet, once they retired, were able to receive the full benefits available under the law at the time. A classic, widely reported example is the case of the very first social security recipient, Ida M. Fuller of Vermont, who paid social security taxes for only three years before she retired in 1940.[2] By that time, she and her employer had paid a total of only $44 in payroll taxes. Yet she collected social

[2]Martin S. Feldstein, "National Saving in the United States," Harvard Institute of Economic Research Discussion Paper no. 506 (Cambridge, Mass., October 1976); idem, "Toward a Reform of Social Security," *Public Interest* (Summer 1975): 75–95; idem, "The Optimal Financing of Social Security," Harvard Institute of Economic Research Discussion Paper no. 388 (Cambridge, Mass., November 1974). Studies by others have found returns in about the same range. See J. A. Stockfish, "Measuring the Social Rate of Return on Private Investment," in *Discounting for Time and Risk in Energy Policy*, ed. Robert C. Lind (Washington: Resources for the Future, 1982); D. M. Holland and S. Myers, "Trends in Corporate Profitability and Capital Costs," in *The Nation's Capital Needs*, ed. R. Lindsay (New York: Committee for Economic Development, 1979), pp. 103–89; W. D. Nordhaus, "The Falling Share of Profits," *Brookings Papers on Economic Activity*, vol. 2 (Washington: Brookings Institution, 1974), pp. 169–208; J. A. Gorman, "Nonfinancial Corporations: New Measures of Output and Input," *Survey of Current Business* (March 1974); J. A. Stockfish, *The Planning-Programming-Budgeting System: Progress and Potentials, Hearings before the Subcommittee on Economy in Government*, Joint Economic Committee (Washington: Government Printing Office, September 1967), pp. 133–43.

security retirement benefits for the next 35 years, until she died in 1975 at the age of 100. During that period she received $20,884.52 in benefits, an enormous return on the taxes she and her employer paid into the program.

Over the years, as workers retired who paid the program's taxes for more of their careers, the rate of return paid by social security has fallen, precisely as our analysis would indicate. Today's retirees are receiving much less of a good deal than the earliest retirees such as Ida Fuller, but they are still receiving above-market returns. Because social security in the United States was, in effect, phased in, rather than adopted in full from the start, the start-up phase with its above-market returns has been stretched out, and the windfall returns of the earlier retirees have also been somewhat lower than they otherwise would have been. The periodic benefit increases during the phase-in process may also have occasionally disrupted the otherwise steady decline of returns paid by the program. But the general pattern and long-term trend have been as described above.

Social security's returns will continue to fall until the mature phase is reached, which will certainly have arrived by the time today's young workers retire.

The Mature Phase

The operation of a public pay-as-you-go system in the mature phase can best be understood by contrasting it with that of a private fully funded system. The money paid into a fully funded system is saved and invested, and returned to each individual in retirement. The capital investments made through this system actually increase production, and the value of this production increase is returned to investors in the form of a rate of return or interest payment on their investments. Over the course of a lifetime, this return would generally accumulate to huge amounts, providing individuals with large estates to support their retirement years, assuming payments into the system equivalent to social security taxes today. The returns accumulated in these large estates would allow individuals to receive far more in retirement benefits than the simple dollar amounts they paid into the system over the years, all due to the increased production.

But a pay-as-you-go system like social security, where essentially no funds are saved and invested, adds nothing to production. It just transfers funds from one segment of the population to another.

15

This means that individuals under such a system lose the full amount of the increased production and associated returns they would get if their money were invested in private, productive assets through a fully funded system. They lose the huge accumulation of assets and large estates that would finance retirement benefits under a fully funded system. Since the pay-as-you-go system does nothing to increase production, each retiree can get no more out of the program in benefits than the simple amounts paid in taxes, unless the government increases the taxes it collects from the following generation of workers to pay his generation increased benefits.

Thus, the essential difference between the private fully funded system and the public pay-as-you-go system is that the former relies on wealth creation while the latter relies on mere income redistribution. Because of this difference, a fully funded system will generally be able to pay much higher benefits than a mature pay-as-you-go system.

The total return earned through the fully funded system is the before-tax, real rate of return to capital. According to Martin Feldstein and others, this return in the United States has historically been at least 12 to 13 percent in real terms. This return signifies the total amount of benefits produced by such a system. Even if some of this return is taxed away, that just means that some of the benefits are being used to purchase government goods and services, rather than being channeled entirely into retirement income. But the new tax revenues, and the government goods and services purchased with them, are still to be counted as part of the benefits produced by the fully funded system.

The before-tax real rate of return to capital is therefore the most appropriate measure to use when comparing the returns under a fully funded system with those under a pay-as-you-go system like social security. This comparison is most appropriate also because social security's returns are always analyzed on an untaxed basis. Indeed, the program produces no tax revenues for non–social security expenditures in any event. Our empirical examination of social security returns below will focus entirely on before-tax returns.[3]

---

[3]This discussion in particular does not involve any reduction in returns due to the recently adopted taxation of social security benefits (see chap. 2), even though such taxation is more a cut in benefits than a true tax, since the revenues do not go into the general fund to purchase other government goods and services, but rather are returned to social security itself.

As we have noted, in a mature pay-as-you-go system no real return at all can be paid except to the extent that tax revenues increase over time. There are, however, two factors that naturally tend to produce increased revenues over time at fixed payroll tax rates, thereby allowing a mature, stable, pay-as-you-go system to pay some real return,[4] though as we shall see this return is qualitatively different from that produced by a fully funded system.

The first of these factors is the rate of growth in real wages. As real wages (the tax base) increase over time, the total revenue collected through a fixed tax rate on those wages (the payroll tax) increases by the rate of such wage growth. The second factor is the rate of growth of the working population. As this population grows, the total tax collected through a fixed tax rate on the wages of this larger number of people grows by the rate of such population growth as well.

In all, because of these two factors, total tax revenue produced by a fixed payroll tax rate increases over time by the rate of growth in real wages plus the rate of growth in the working population. In a pure pay-as-you-go system, where all taxes collected are paid out in benefits each year, the real benefits that can be paid are increased annually by the sum of these two rates. This sum consequently represents the real return in a mature pay-as-you-go system. An individual who pays taxes into a mature, stable, pay-as-you-go program all of his life will receive back his tax money cumulatively increased by this real rate of return.

Under prevailing economic and demographic conditions this mature pay-as-you-go return is quite low. The rate of growth in real wages over the past four decades has been less than 1.5 percent.[5] Furthermore, at current fertility rates, the working population

---

[4]A precise mathematical presentation of this analysis was provided in Henry J. Aaron, "The Social Insurance Paradox," *Canadian Journal of Economics* 32 (February–November 1966): 371–74.

[5]The rate of growth in real wages from 1952 to 1975 was 1.3 percent. See Martin Feldstein, "Facing the Social Security Crisis," Harvard Institute of Economic Research Discussion Paper no. 492 (Cambridge, Mass., July 1976). From 1952 to 1977, this average was 1.37 percent (based on data from the Social Security Administration). Since then, real wage growth has been no higher and has even been sharply negative in some years.

will eventually be declining rather than increasing.[6] This decline could easily overwhelm the effects of the increase in real wages, making the overall pay-as-you-go real rate of return negative. Even if long-standing fertility trends did reverse themselves, their current strength and the strong social forces behind them make it unlikely that the working population would grow enough in the foreseeable future to add substantially to the pay-as-you-go rate of return.

Even in the very best of times, experience indicates that the mature pay-as-you-go real rate of return will never amount to more than a minor fraction of the before-tax real rate of return to capital earned in a fully funded system. A prolonged period of 2 percent real wage growth and 2 percent growth in the working population— which would be quite remarkable—would at best produce a pay-as-you-go return only one-third as large as the full before-tax return to capital.

Consequently, once the pay-as-you-go rate of return falls to its steady state in the mature stage, it will have fallen well below the rate earned in a fully funded system. A private fully funded system, therefore, can generally pay much higher benefits than a pay-as-you system in the mature phase. This will be especially so for social security in the foreseeable future, given the prevailing adverse economic and demographic conditions in the United States for such a system.

Moreover, regardless of the level of the mature pay-as-you-go rate of return, this return is qualitatively different from the return generated in a fully funded system. Returns under the fully funded system are financed by the increased production resulting from the system itself. They are, therefore, self-financing and do not constitute a burden to anyone. Any return paid through a mature pay-as-you-go system, however, is generated merely by increased taxes, without any increased production to pay for it. Such a return, therefore, constitutes a burden on current workers. It is the result

[6]The fertility rate for 1982 was 1.86, as cited in the *1984 Annual Report of the Board of Trustees of the Federal Old-Age and Survivors Insurance and Disability Insurance Trust Funds* (Washington: Government Printing Office, April 5, 1984). (Hereafter the annual trustees reports for OASDI will be cited as in this example: *1984 OASDI Report.*) To maintain a constant population, the fertility rate must be 2.1. Though fertility rates for the last 10 years have been stable or even slightly increasing, they have followed a persistent long-term downward trend for almost 200 years. See Peter J. Ferrara, *Social Security: The Inherent Contradiction* (Washington: Cato Institute, 1980), table 33.

18

only of redistribution, and consequently retirees are being made better off only by making workers worse off. Under the pay-as-you-go system, regardless of the returns offered in the mature phase, workers over the generations still lose the entire amount of newly created wealth represented by the rate of return in a fully funded system.

It should also be noted that even the transitory above-market returns available during the start-up phase of a pay-as-you-go system are the result not of increased production but of increased taxation on the first generation of workers. Such returns therefore result simply from making this first generation of workers worse off through the appropriation and redistribution of a substantial portion of their incomes. To the extent that these returns were above market rates, they in fact constituted a simple welfare subsidy to all eligible social security beneficiaries in the first generation of retirees, regardless of need. Such indiscriminate payment of welfare subsidies should be considered an unconscionable waste of scarce taxpayer resources. Moreover, the high returns of the start-up phase are payable only at the cost of imposing the inferior, mature phase on all future generations.

In any event, even accepting social security's pay-as-you-go returns at face value our analysis indicates that workers under the mature phase of the program, such as those entering the work force today, will receive low, below-market returns on the taxes paid into it and consequently will receive far lower benefits than they would under a private fully funded system with its much higher returns.

Social Security's Returns for Today's Young Workers

In order to analyze the returns offered by social security to today's young workers, we focused on 12 different hypothetical families composed of workers entering the work force:

1. Single worker, earns the minimum wage each year for entire career, never marries, no children;
2. Single worker, earns the average income for all workers in social security–covered employment each year for entire career, never marries, no children;
3. Single worker, earns maximum social security–taxable income each year for entire career, never marries, no children;
4. Married couple, one spouse works and earns minimum wage

for entire career, other spouse does not work, children as described below;

5. Married couple, both spouses work and earn minimum wage for entire careers, children as described below;

6. Married couple, one spouse works and earns average income in social security–covered employment each year for entire career, other spouse does not work, children as described below;

7. Married couple, one spouse works and earns average income in social security–covered employment each year for entire career, other spouse works and earns minimum wage for entire career, children as described below;

8. Married couple, both spouses work and earn average income in social security–covered employment for entire careers, children as described below;

9. Married couple, one spouse works and earns maximum social security–taxable income each year for entire career, other spouse does not work, children as described below;

10. Married couple, one spouse works and earns maximum social security–taxable income each year for entire career, other spouse works and earns minimum wage for entire career, children as described below;

11. Married couple, one spouse works and earns maximum social security–taxable income each year for entire career, other spouse works and earns average income in social security–covered employment for entire career, children as described below;

12. Married couple, both spouses work and earn maximum social security–taxable income each year for entire careers, children as described below.

All workers were assumed to start working in 1983. Low-income career workers were assumed to be 18 in that year, average-income career workers were assumed to be 22, and maximum-income career workers were assumed to be 24. All married workers were assumed to marry the year they started working and to retire at age 67, the normal social security retirement age for today's young workers under current law. Married couples were assumed to have one child when the oldest worker reached 26, and another child when the oldest worker reached 28. All other assumptions were taken from the Alternative IIB set of assumptions in the 1983 annual social security trustees report.[7]

For each of these families, we calculated the amount that wage earners and their employers would have to pay in OASDI taxes throughout the workers' careers. We next calculated the expected social security benefits provided each family in return. In addition to retirement benefits, this included survivors benefits (multiplied by the probability of death in each year), and disability benefits (multiplied by the probability of becoming disabled in each year). We then determined the rate of return represented by benefits for each family in relation to the taxes paid for that family.

It should be noted that this calculation does not require any assumption regarding the appropriate discount rate or market rate of return. It simply determines the rate of return paid by social security to different hypothetical families, and this return can be compared with various market interest rates and returns.

The 12 different hypothetical family combinations studied cover a broad spectrum of possibilities. The vast majority of young workers entering the work force today will receive returns from social security within the range of returns received by these hypothetical families.

Our results actually overestimate the true social security rates of return for these families for two reasons. First, for simplicity we assumed that once a worker became disabled, he remained disabled until retirement. In actuality, disabled workers eligible for social security often recover after a few years and then return to the work force, where they begin paying taxes again and stop receiving benefits. This simplifying assumption consequently increased the expected value of promised benefits and reduced the expected cost of social security taxes, increasing the program's estimated rates of return.

Second, we did not account for the new income taxation of social security retirement benefits adopted by the 1983 legislation to save the program from bankruptcy. Projected returns were not reduced by the amount of such taxation, which will apply to virtually all retirees by the time today's young workers retire. This taxation of social security benefits has a peculiar aspect to it indicating that it should be viewed as a reduction in benefits rather than as the generation of new tax revenues: all income tax revenues generated

[7] *1983 OASDI Report* (June 24, 1983).

by this taxation are to be funneled back into social security itself and cannot be used to finance other government programs. Consequently, the untaxed social security benefits do not represent the full amount of income available to workers either for direct consumption or for the purchase of government services (through taxation). Rather, only the portion remaining after federal income taxation is so available, as the taxed-away portion is recycled within the program to service existing benefit obligations.

Consequently, the full benefits provided by social security for workers are only the benefits left after federal income taxation. By counting the entire, untaxed amount of benefits in our calculations, we again increase the estimated social security rate of return above what in our view should be considered the true rate.

The results of our calculations are presented in Table 1, arranged from the family combination having the lowest return to the one having the highest return. These results indicate that all the families with maximum-income workers, whether such workers are single or married, whether or not they have children, and regardless of the income of any spouse, are promised zero or negative real rates of return through social security. Single workers are promised an

---

Table 1

SOCIAL SECURITY REAL RATES OF RETURN FOR DIFFERENT
FAMILY COMBINATIONS

Family Combinations[1]	Real Rate of Return (%)
Single maximum-income worker (3)	−1.5
Two maximum-income spouses (12)	−1.0
Maximum-income spouse, average-income spouse (11)	−0.5
Maximum-income spouse, low-income spouse (10)	−0.5
Maximum-income spouse, nonworking spouse (9)	0.0
Single average-income worker (2)	0.0
Two average-income spouses (8)	0.5
Average-income spouse, low-income spouse (7)	1.0
Average-income spouse, nonworking spouse (6)	1.5
Two low-income spouses (5)	1.5
Single low-income worker (1)	1.5
Low-income spouse, nonworking spouse (4)	2.75

[1]Numbers in parentheses refer to family combinations described on pp. 19–20.

average of zero real returns. The great majority of two-earner couples are promised a real return of 1 percent or less, with only two-career minimum-wage spouses receiving a 1.5 percent real return. Recognizing that two-earner couples will predominate among workers currently starting their careers, these results can be summarized as indicating that for most of these young workers, the real rate of return promised by social security is 1 percent or less, and for many it is zero or even negative.

Returns on Private Market Investments

These social security returns are far below widely available market returns. Addressing the issue of possible private sector returns on retirement investments, Martin Feldstein wrote in 1976:

> Over the past twenty-five years, the real annual yield after adjusting for inflation was 8 percent for common stocks and 3 percent for corporate bonds. A conservative portfolio with half of each would have yielded 5.5%.[8]

Indeed, if half the annual payments into an investment pool were invested each year in common stocks with an 8 percent real return and half in corporate bonds with a 3 percent real return, and the return on each half were reinvested in stocks and bonds respectively, then the real average annual yield after 41 years would be 6.5 percent.

Similarly, economist Robert S. Kaplan of Carnegie-Mellon University considered the returns on private investments relative to returns through social security in a paper presented at an American Enterprise Institute conference in 1977. Kaplan wrote:

> Even including the poor performance of the stock market in the past ten years, the long-term rate of return on equity investments has averaged more than 6 or 7 percentage points above the rate of inflation. Thus, as individuals are forced to provide more of their retirement income from social security, they are also being forced to invest in a program whose real rate of return is far below what could be earned through a private retirement program.[9]

---

[8]Feldstein, "Facing the Social Security Crisis."

[9]Robert S. Kaplan, "A Comparison of Rates of Return to Social Security Retirees Under Wage and Price Indexing," in *Financing Social Security*, ed. Colin D. Campbell (Washington, American Enterprise Institute, 1979).

Over the postwar period, 1946 to 1983, the average combined real rate of return on all stocks on the New York Stock Exchange was 6.9 percent.[10] If we go all the way back before the Great Depression, taking the period 1926 to 1983, this return was 6.4 percent.[11] These returns represent after-tax returns remaining after corporate income taxes, payroll taxes, property taxes, state and local income taxes, and other taxes have been paid at the corporate level. Such returns are consequently not inconsistent with the full, real, before-tax return on capital investment of 12 percent discussed earlier. Indeed, in addition to the above after-tax returns, the private investments would also yield new tax revenues to finance government services, an additional benefit accounting generally for the remainder of the full before-tax returns.

These returns over such long periods of time indicate the stable long-run returns one could routinely expect on such investments in the future. Moreover, a worker investing in a broadly based basket of most or all such stocks, roughly holding for all practical purposes a piece of the economy as a whole, would face no greater risk than the chance of the collapse of the entire economy, a risk to which social security would be even more vulnerable. These returns, with such thoroughly minimized risk, are easily available to average investors through Individual Retirement Accounts (IRAs) or similar vehicles simply by using the funds in such vehicles to purchase shares in broad pools of equity investments, such as mutual funds.[12]

[10]Roger G. Ibbotson and Rex A. Sinquefeld, *Stocks, Bonds, Bills and Inflation Quarterly Service* 1, no. 2 (July 1983).

[11]Ibid.

[12]If workers were allowed to substitute fully funded private IRAs for social security, a huge increase in savings could result. Such an increase in savings and investment supply would tend to lower interest rates and investment returns across the whole economy, including the return on private retirement investments.

But returns would be reduced only to the extent that there was an actual increase in savings. This increase would be limited to the degree to which workers individually chose the IRA option. Moreover, the option would naturally rebate taxes to workers who chose the IRAs over social security (or else there would be no real option at all). Any resulting savings increase would be offset to the extent that the government responded to the revenue loss by increasing borrowing.

Moreover, the impact on returns depends on the actual empirical sensitivity of such returns to any particular level of savings increase (i.e., the elasticity of capital returns). In an economy as large and open as that of the United States, it is difficult to move a fundamental element like returns to capital to a significant degree. Any impact on such returns due to increased saving would be especially mitigated due to the heavy integration of the U.S. economy with international capital markets, diluting any U.S. savings increase in the huge pool of international capital.

Though some commentators have challenged the accuracy of the figures quoted above (and discussed in earlier works)[13] for private investment returns, such criticism is without foundation and is itself clearly in error. Retired former social security chief actuary Robert Myers repeatedly states, for example, that such returns would be well above historical trends for "the interest rate." But there is no single "interest rate"; rather, there are numerous interest rates and returns in the marketplace. Myers in fact seems to be referring to the interest rate on the securities held by the program's trust funds, which is prospectively estimated each year in the assumptions used by the Board of Trustees for the trust funds to project their future financial health. But these are special securities issued by the federal government for social security alone, with a return indexed to certain Treasury bill rates. Clearly, this return does not involve returns earned on broadly based equity investments, which are an entirely different matter. No critic, including Myers, has ever challenged the sources cited for the returns quoted above, which include standard sources routinely cited for such data. No critic has ever offered contrasting data from other sources. The returns discussed above are the historical returns on equity investments, and this information is readily available in any library.

With such market returns, those entering the work force today would clearly receive several times the benefits offered by social security if they could invest over their careers in IRA-type vehicles the amounts they and their employers are currently required to pay into social security in payroll taxes. To illustrate this we calculated

---

Finally, the high level of real interest around the world over the last several years suggests a relative scarcity of capital as compared with earlier years. Any U.S. savings increase may well just offset this scarcity, bringing returns closer to historical levels.

These factors suggest that any impact on private capital returns resulting from an option to substitute IRAs for social security would not substantially offset the enormous relative advantage private investments would otherwise appear to have over social security. Any such impact may indeed be miniscule. Of course, any return to capital higher than the social security returns discussed earlier would mean higher benefits through the private IRA investments than through social security.

It should also be recognized that in evaluating the overall appeal of an IRA option, workers are likely to view increased savings and capital and lower interest costs during working years as further beneficial effects of the reform. Increased savings and capital would also tend to increase the marginal productivity of labor and hence wages, providing a further benefit for workers.

[13]See, e.g., Ferrara, *The Inherent Contradiction.*

the amount of such private benefits for six of our hypothetical family combinations, beginning with the amount of OASDI taxes paid by each worker and his employer each year for his entire career. We then assumed that these amounts were invested in an IRA-type vehicle annually, further accumulating investment returns each year. We subtracted from the accumulated sums the expected value of promised social security survivors and disability benefits, assuming that workers would have to use some of their invested funds to purchase life and disability insurance of such value. Eventually we reached the total accumulated sum each worker would have at retirement. We then calculated the retirement benefits such a sum could pay. We assumed throughout that the private investments earned a 6 percent real rate of return, based on the historical investment returns discussed above.

The results are presented in Table 2. All figures are in constant 1983 dollars, so they will not be depreciated by inflation. It is noteworthy that this in effect means that the private benefits in nominal terms would receive the same annual cost of living adjustment increases as social security. The amount of accumulated assets at retirement in the IRA vehicle for each family is shown in the first column of data. The second column, labeled "Perpetual Annuity," shows the amount of benefits that could be paid out of the continuing returns from the assets alone, leaving the assets themselves intact to pass on to children or other heirs. The next two columns, labeled "Life Annuity," indicate the amount of benefits that could be paid if the accumulated assets were to be entirely consumed over the retirement period, leaving nothing for heirs. These annuity benefit values were adjusted to pay more while both spouses were alive than with only one alive, matching the pattern of social security benefits. For the two-earner couples in our hypothetical families, this means that twice the benefits would be paid with both spouses alive as with only one alive. For one-earner couples, this means that 50 percent more would be paid with both spouses alive as with only one alive. The last two columns show the amount of benefits that social security would pay to each family.

The results indicate that two career maximum-income spouses would retire with total accumulated retirement fund assets of $1,759,144 in 1983 dollars. This fund would pay them $105,549 in interest alone each year until both spouses died, allowing them to leave the entire fund of almost $2 million to their children or other heirs. This annual benefit is 4 times the annual benefit of $27,521

Table 2

PRIVATE MARKET BENEFITS vs. SOCIAL SECURITY BENEFITS FOR DIFFERENT FAMILY COMBINATIONS[1]

Family Combinations[2]	Accumulated Assets at Retirement	Perpetual Annuity	Life Annuity		Social Security Pays	
			Both Spouses Alive	One Spouse Alive	Both Spouses Alive	One Spouse Alive
Two maximum-income spouses (12)	1,759,144	105,549	199,115	99,558	27,521	13,761
Maximum-income spouse, nonworking spouse (9)	907,206	54,432	88,357	58,905	20,641	13,761
Two average-income spouses (8)	864,265	51,856	97,824	48,912	19,064	9,532
Average-income spouse, nonworking spouse (6)	448,752	26,925	43,706	29,137	14,298	9,532
Two low-income spouses (5)	531,625	31,898	60,173	30,087	15,326	7,663
Low-income spouse, nonworking spouse (4)	275,243	16,515	26,807	17,871	9,354	6,236

[1] All figures in constant 1983 dollars, market benefits calculated assuming a 6 percent real rate of return
[2] Numbers in parentheses refer to family combinations described on pp. 19–20.

that social security would pay while both spouses were alive and 8 times the annual benefit of $13,761 that the program would pay with only one spouse alive. Alternatively, the retired couple could receive a life annuity paying $199,115 annually with both spouses alive and $99,558 annually with only one spouse alive, about 8 times the social security–promised benefits.

A maximum-income worker with a nonworking spouse would accumulate $907,206 by retirement, which would pay $54,432 in interest alone, almost 3 times the $20,641 that social security would pay with both spouses alive and 4 times the $13,761 that the program would pay with one spouse alive, all while leaving the almost $1 million fund for children or other heirs. Alternatively, the retired worker could receive a life annuity paying $88,357 with both spouses alive and $58,905 with one spouse alive, about 4.5 times what social security would pay.

The benefits and annuities of maximum-income workers with working spouses earning less than maximum incomes would range proportionately between the levels given in these two examples. Single maximum-income workers would receive private benefits relative to those of social security in roughly the same ratio as for two maximum-income spouses, though accumulated assets by retirement and annual private benefits for these workers would be about half of those for the two-earner family.

Two average-income spouses would retire with a trust fund of $864,265, paying them perpetually $51,856 each year in interest. This would allow them to receive 2.5 times the social security–promised benefits of $19,064 with both alive and 5 times the program's benefits of $9,532 with only one alive, all while leaving the almost $1 million retirement fund to children or other heirs. The alternative life annuity would pay these spouses about 5 times what social security would pay.

An average-income worker with a nonworking spouse would retire with a fund of $448,752, paying $26,925 each year out of returns alone, about twice the social security–promised benefits of $14,298 with both alive and 3 times the program's benefits of $9,532 with only one alive, again while still leaving the accumulated retirement fund of almost half a million dollars to heirs. The alternative life annuity would pay these spouses about 3 times what social security would pay.

The benefits and annuities of average-income workers with working spouses earning less than average incomes would again range between the levels indicated in the last two examples. Returns accruing to average-income workers with spouses earning more than average incomes would range between the levels indicated in the examples of the two average-income workers and the two maximum-income workers. Single workers with average incomes would receive private benefits relative to those of social security in a proportion similar to that received by the family with two average-income spouses, with accumulated assets and private benefits in absolute terms about half as much as for the two-earner family.

Finally, two career minimum-wage spouses would retire with accumulated assets of $531,625. This would pay them $31,898 annually out of interest alone, about twice the social security benefits of $15,326 with both alive and 4.5 times the program's benefits of $7,663 with one alive. At the same time, the entire one-half million dollar trust fund would be left to children or other heirs, providing a sturdy foundation for their economic advancement. Alternatively, these workers could receive a life annuity paying about 4 times hat social security would pay. A single low-income worker would receive a ratio of private benefits similar to that provided by social security, though on an approximately 50 percent reduced scale.

The career minimum-wage earner with a nonworking spouse is offered the best deal from social security. But through the private system, such a worker could still retire with accumulated assets of $275,243. Annual returns alone would pay the worker and his spouse $16,515 each year in benefits, about 75 percent more than the social security benefits of $9,354 with both alive and 2.5 times the program's benefits of $6,236 with one alive, all while allowing them to leave one-quarter million dollars to their children or other heirs. Alternatively, worker and spouse could receive a life annuity paying about 2.5 times what social security would pay.

Overall, these results indicate that most young workers entering the work force today could receive 3 to 6 times the retirement benefits promised through social security, if they could invest the program's mandated payroll taxes in a private IRA-type vehicle and earn the above-discussed market returns. A similar comprehensive study published in 1980 reached the same results.[14] Of course, lower returns on private investments would still yield benefits much higher than those available through social security, though not so much more as in the examples above. Indeed, any private returns higher

[14]Ferrara, *The Inherent Contradiction*, chap. 4.

Table 3
PRIVATE MARKET BENEFITS VS. SOCIAL SECURITY BENEFITS AT DIFFERENT INVESTMENT RETURNS[1]

Family Combinations	Assumed Real Return (%)	Accumulated Assets at Retirement	Perpetual Annuity	Life Annuity		Social Security Pays	
				Both Spouses Alive	One Spouse Alive	Both Spouses Alive	One Spouse Alive
Two maximum-income spouses (12)	5.5	1,534,130	84,377	167,917	83,958	27,521	13,761
	5.0	1,340,695	67,035	141,767	70,884	27,521	13,761
	4.5	1,174,241	52,841	119,837	59,919	27,521	13,761
	4.0	1,030,873	41,235	101,435	50,718	27,521	13,761
Maximum-income spouse, nonworking spouse (9)	5.5	791,803	43,549	74,220	49,480	20,641	13,761
	5.0	692,477	34,624	62,398	41,598	20,641	13,761
	4.5	606,896	27,310	52,505	35,004	20,641	13,761
	4.0	533,085	21,323	44,227	29,484	20,641	13,761
Two average-income spouses (8)	5.5	746,949	41,082	81,756	40,878	19,064	9,532
	5.0	646,995	32,350	68,414	34,207	19,064	9,532
	4.5	561,742	25,278	57,329	28,665	19,064	9,532
	4.0	488,957	19,558	48,111	24,056	19,064	9,532
Average-income spouse, nonworking spouse (6)	5.5	388,207	21,351	36,389	24,259	14,298	9,532
	5.0	336,536	16,827	30,325	20,216	14,298	9,532
	4.5	292,386	13,157	25,296	16,864	14,298	9,532
	4.0	254,620	10,185	21,124	14,083	14,298	9,532

Table 3 (cont.)

Family Combinations	Assumed Real Return (%)	Accumulated Assets at Retirement	Perpetual Annuity	Life Annuity		Social Security Pays	
				Both Spouses Alive	One Spouse Alive	Both Spouses Alive	One Spouse Alive
Two low-income spouses (5)	5.5	452,334	24,878	49,509	24,755	15,326	7,663
	5.0	385,877	19,294	40,804	20,402	15,326	7,663
	4.5	330,111	14,855	33,689	16,845	15,326	7,663
	4.0	283,259	11,330	27,872	13,936	15,326	7,663
Low-income spouse, nonworking spouse (4)	5.5	234,282	12,886	21,961	14,640	9,354	6,236
	5.0	199,877	9,994	18,010	12,007	9,354	6,236
	4.5	170,938	7,692	14,789	9,860	9,354	6,236
	4.0	146,564	5,863	12,160	8,107	9,354	6,236

[1]Dollar figures in constant 1983 dollars.
[2]Numbers in parentheses refer to family combinations described on pp. 19–20.

31

than the social security returns discussed earlier would result in higher benefits through the private investment system than through social security. This is illustrated in Table 3, which presents the results of calculations as above at lower assumed real rates of return.

In addition to the above benefits, there would also be the new tax revenues produced by the private retirement investments, which would be available to finance government goods and services or tax cuts. As noted earlier, this is a further benefit of the private system not produced by social security, since the program produces no tax revenues for non–social security expenditures. If the taxed-away portion of before-tax returns is equal to four percentage points and if those entering the work force today invested in private systems throughout their careers the same amounts they and their employers would otherwise be required to pay in social security payroll taxes, then by the time these workers retired more than enough new tax revenue would be produced each year to finance an entire national defense budget of the same size relative to GNP as today's.

Conclusion

Our empirical results confirm our theoretical analysis. While those retired today are still receiving above-market returns through social security, those now entering the work force are offered low, below-market returns, in many cases negative, even if all the program's promised benefits are paid. The high returns previously paid through social security explain in large part the past popularity of the program. But as today's young workers come to understand the bad deal offered to them by the program, the impact on the politics of social security is likely to be revolutionary, creating substantial prospects for real, fundamental reform.

While the public undoubtedly still remembers the recent social security financial crisis faced by the Reagan administration, many are hoping the public has already forgotten that the program had to be rescued from financial collapse just a short time earlier during the Carter years. In December 1977, Carter and the Congress enacted into law a social security rescue package based on the largest peacetime tax increase in U.S. history. At that time President Carter, the Social Security Administration (SSA), and the rest of the program's establishment old guard, promised the American people that the system would be financially secure "for the rest of this century and well into the next one."[1]

By the time Reagan entered office in 1981, however, social security was already again in deep financial trouble. The *1980 OASDI Report* had concluded that the system would soon be unable to pay its benefits when due, possibly as early as late 1981, even under the relatively optimistic "intermediate" assumptions.[2] While under these projections the crisis could possibly be averted by allowing the retirement benefits trust fund to borrow from the disability and health insurance trust funds, under the so-called pessimistic assumptions even that would not be enough.[3] Historically, reality has generally turned out to be at least as bad as the "pessimistic" projections indicated. In this case reality turned out even worse in the short term. For the long term, the *1980 OASDI Report* also projected a large shortfall of social security revenues.[4]

A few months after Reagan entered office, the *1981 OASDI Report* showed that even under the intermediate assumptions, and with complete borrowing among the system's trust funds, the program would still soon be unable to pay promised benefits. The long-term revenue shortfall had also increased substantially in just one year.[5]

[1]See, e.g., the *1978 OASDI Report* (May 15, 1978), p. 3.

[2]*1980 OASDI Report* (June 17, 1980).

[3]Ibid.

[4]Ibid.

[5]*1981 OASDI Report* (July 2, 1981).

In May 1981, the administration responded to the impending crisis by proposing a package of changes in the program based entirely on benefit reductions. President Reagan had promised during the 1980 campaign that he would not cut social security benefits for present retirees, and the administration's proposal fundamentally kept that pledge. The only element that affected current retirees was a one-time permanent three-month delay in COLA increases.

The major feature of the package for the short term was a reduction in benefits for workers who chose early retirement in the future, though full benefits would still be available to those who waited until age 65 to retire. The major feature for the long term was a temporary change in the formula used to calculate increases in future benefits for today's workers, which would result in an eventual 10 percent cut in expected benefits for those retiring in the next century, though benefits would still have been higher in real terms than today.

The proposed reforms met with a firestorm of criticism. Democrats clearly viewed the proposal as an opportunity to destroy Reagan's broad popularity at the time. Social security's old guard flatly denied that the program was in any danger at all, on the strategy that the longer a rescue package was delayed, the more any possible benefit cuts as the solution would have to be sudden and preemptory, thus making it less likely that such cuts would be adopted. But the Republican-controlled Senate dealt Reagan the harshest blow of his administration over the issue. It passed a resolution on a 96–0 vote advising the president not even to send the proposed reform package to Capitol Hill.

The Senate action killed the administration's proposal, foreclosing even rational debate. Instead, Reagan reached an interim compromise with Congress. Legislation would be immediately enacted allowing social security's trust funds to borrow from each other as needed, which would enable the system to continue paying benefits on time until after the 1982 elections. At the same time, a bipartisan commission would be named to recommend changes necessary to prevent the system's financial collapse. President Reagan, House Speaker Tip O'Neill, and Senate Majority Leader Howard Baker would each choose five commission members, and the commission would report its recommendations right after the 1982 elections.

O'Neill named Rep. Claude Pepper (D-Fla.), former social security commissioner Robert Ball, former Democratic congresswoman Martha Keys, and Reps. Barber Conable (R-N.Y.) and William Archer

(R-Tex.). Baker named AFL-CIO president Lane Kirkland, and Sens. Daniel Patrick Moynihan (D-N.Y.), Robert Dole (R-Kans.), John Heinz (R-Pa.), and William Armstrong (R-Colo.). The president named Alan Greenspan, chairman of the Council of Economic Advisers under President Ford; Robert Beck, head of Prudential Insurance Company; Alexander Trowbridge, president of the National Association of Manufacturers; former Democratic congressman Joe Waggoner; and management consultant Mary Falvey Fuller. Greenspan was to serve as commission chairman. Robert Myers, former chief actuary of the Social Security Administration, was named executive director of the commission, responsible for providing technical background information.

It was clear from the moment the commission members were named that the old guard establishment was firmly in control and that no fundamental reform of social security would even be considered. Archliberals Pepper, Ball, and Kirkland, backed up by Moynihan and Keys, were prepared to scream "geriatricide" if any fundamental reforms were seriously entertained. The elected politicians on the panel were not about to propose anything new. Armstrong, Archer, and Waggoner showed some spirit, but they were destined from the start for a dissenting minority report. The business representatives on the panel were more interested in appearing to be part of the establishment than in advancing innovative reforms. Chairman Greenspan shunned any intellectual leadership role. That role consequently was filled by Executive Director Myers, a certified old guardsman who had worked at the Social Security Administration for 35 years.

Myers dominated the commission's proceedings. He was in total control of the information flow and defined what was credible and what was not, without challenge. Myers spoonfed the commission all the mythologies, shibboleths, and incantations of the old guard establishment, with Ball and Moynihan in key supporting roles. Myers produced a booklet for the commission listing a large number of tinkering tax and benefit changes in the system, and the funds that would supposedly be raised by each. Thereafter, the commission's discussion was limited to the contents of that booklet.

In the meantime, the commission failed to defuse the social security issue for Reagan and the Republicans. Quite the contrary, the commission heightened the problem. Democrats campaigned across the country on the theme that Republicans were planning to cut social security following the election. The existence at that very time of a presidential commission that would recommend changes right after the election lent crucial credibility to the charge.

By December the commission was still floundering. Myers was able to define the parameters of debate narrowly, but he had no political clout to force a decision. Commission members were merely circling and glowering at each other, like gang members before a brawl. Press accounts suggested that the commission was planning to report in January three separate, alternative reform packages—one each from the group's liberal, moderate, and conservative camps. In the meantime, it appeared that the system would be unable to pay timely benefits by late summer 1983.

At this point the White House stepped in and began closed-door negotiations with certain commission members. Chief of Staff Baker, his aide Richard Darman, and Office of Management and Budget Director David Stockman negotiated primarily with Ball and Moynihan. Greenspan, Conable, and Beck were also included, to ensure that the moderates would go along. House Speaker O'Neill participated through communications with the liberal commissioners.

The White House was anxious for the commission to reach a final decision that would end the issue as a political problem for the president. For its part, the old guard establishment was willing to negotiate because it too was getting nervous. If the commission failed to reach a compromise, the public might turn to consideration of proposals for more fundamental reform, and the old guard might lose control of the debate. Moreover, if political deadlock led to the late payment of social security benefits even for a short while, the credibility of the old guard as to the soundness of the program might be permanently damaged. In the developing climate of panic, anything might happen. For these reasons the old guard not only turned to negotiate with the administration, but even gave in somewhat to White House preferences.

The negotiations produced a package of proposals supported by 12 of the commissioners, with Armstrong, Archer, and Waggoner dissenting. Though Myers was for the most part shut out of the final closed-door negotiations on the grounds that he was staff and not a commission member, and though the details of the final package were not all to his liking, the ultimate recommendations were drawn entirely from his conceptual framework.

The commission's final recommendations are discussed below by A. Haeworth Robertson, a former chief actuary of the Social Security Administration. An updated outlook will be discussed later.

II. The National Commision's Failure to Achieve Real Reform

A. Haeworth Robertson

Introduction

On January 20, 1983, the National Commission on Social Security Reform released its long-awaited report, discharging its mandate to identify social security's financial problems and propose "solutions to such problems that will both assure the financial integrity of the Social Security System and the provision of appropriate benefits."[1] This report was duly presented on February 1, 1983, to the Committee on Ways and Means of the United States House of Representatives.

The work of the National Commission on Social Security Reform was extremely disappointing. Not because it failed to make recommendations that would resolve all of social security's financial and design problems—that would be asking too much. But because it failed to identify and report forcefully the full extent of the problems so that Congress and the public would know that such problems exist. This failure to be honest and forthright with the public, if not corrected, will result in the continued erosion of public confidence—not only in social security but in the government itself.

Summary of Major Provisions

The major provisions of the commission's compromise proposal to resolve social security's financial problems are summarized below.

1. The social security tax rate for both employers and employees was to be set as follows: for 1983, 6.70; 1984, 7.00; 1985, 7.05; 1986–87, 7.15; 1988–89, 7.51; and 1990, 7.65. In effect, this

---

The author was formerly chief actuary of the Social Security Administration and is now managing director of William M. Mercer, Inc.

[1]*Report of the National Commission on Social Security Reform* (Washington: Government Printing Office, January 1983), chap. 1, p. 2.

meant higher taxes in 1984, 1988, and 1989 than scheduled previously. Only in 1984 was the worker to be allowed a refundable tax credit equal to the entire increase (0.30 percent) in social security taxes.

2. The social security tax for OASDI levied on self-employed persons was to be increased from three-fourths of the combined employer-employee rate to the full employer-employee rate. Half of the total payment could be deducted from taxable income for income tax purposes, but not for purposes of determining the OASDI and HI (Hospital Insurance) tax. Many self-employed people would thus pay a higher net amount of social security and income taxes.

3. The annual cost-of-living adjustment, formerly paid in July, was to be postponed for 1983 until January 1984, and then paid each January thereafter. The change was to affect all 36 million beneficiaries. A special provision sought to reduce the impact on low-income elderly and disabled persons who were also receiving welfare payments.

4. Half of a person's social security benefits was to be subject to federal income tax, but only if he had an adjusted gross income of at least $20,000 from sources excluding social security, or in the case of a married couple filing jointly, if they had $25,000. The proceeds of this income tax were to be paid into the OASDI trust funds. Some 3 million people, or about 10 percent of OASDI beneficiaries, would have paid extra taxes under this provision.

5. As of January 1, 1984, mandatory social security coverage was to be extended to all new federal workers. It was also to be extended to all employees of nonprofit organizations, for whom participation was previously optional. Federal workers who were covered by the Civil Service Retirement System were not to be affected. It was anticipated that the government would establish a supplementary employer pension for new federal employees, so they would end up receiving social security plus a supplementary pension (as is now the case with many private-sector workers).

6. Local and state governments covered by social security were to be prohibited from opting out as of the date of enactment of the proposed plan, unless the process of termination was completed by such date.

7. The so-called windfall portion of social security benefits received

by federal, state, and local government employees qualifying for social security on the basis of relatively short periods of employment in the private sector was to be eliminated, starting with those eligible to retire after 1983. They would receive a benefit, but less than previously.

8. Beginning in 1988, whenever the combined OASDI trust funds dropped to less than one-fifth of a year's benefits, the annual COLA increase was to be set to equal the annual rise in either prices or wages, whichever was less.

9. From 1990 to 2010, a larger bonus was to be phased in, equal to 8 percent a year instead of the current 3 percent, for each year a person delays retirement after age 65 and before age 70.

10. The trust fund was to be reimbursed by the Treasury for free wage credits granted to military personnel in the past and for uncashed social security checks.

11. Benefits and eligibility were to be improved for certain categories of widows and widowers, divorced persons, and survivors.

12. In the case of salary-reduction plans qualifying under Section 401(k) of the Internal Revenue Code, any salary reduction thereunder was not to be treated as a reduction in the wages subject to OASDI taxes.

Financial Aspects of the Recommendations

How effective are the recommendations in resolving social security's financial problems? Unfortunately, not very.

During its meetings on November 11–13, 1982, the commission adopted a background book of actuarial cost estimates for OASDI and HI. These estimates defined the size and scope of social security's financial problems as follows.

- During the 1983–89 period, provision will have to be made to increase OASDI income or to decrease benefits, or some combination of both, by $150 billion to $200 billion (that is, by 9 to 12 percent of projected OASDI expenditures).
- During the 75 years from 1982 to 2056, the average annual OASDI deficit (defined by comparing income and outgo according to the IIB intermediate demographic and economic assumptions used in the *1982 OASDI Report*), will be equal to average annual expenditures of 14.09 percent of taxable payroll and

39

average annual tax income of 12.27 percent of taxable payroll. This will yield an average annual deficit of 1.82 percent of taxable payroll.

- During the 1983–89 period, scheduled taxes will be barely adequate to pay HI benefits; increased taxes or decreased benefits for HI must be adopted no later than 1990. Under less optimistic assumptions, this remedial action must be taken in the late 1980s, and even sooner if OASDI continues to borrow from HI.
- During the 75 years from 1982 to 2056, the average annual HI deficit (defined by comparing income and outgo according to the IIB intermediate demographic and economic assumptions used in the *1982 HI Report*), will be equal to average annual expenditures of 8.10 percent of taxable payroll and average annual tax income of 2.89 percent of taxable payroll. This will yield an average annual deficit of 5.21 percent of taxable payroll.

The commission's recommendations attempted to assure the near-term solvency of the OASDI program by increasing projected net income during the 1983–89 period by $169 billion (by increasing taxes by $129 billion and decreasing projected benefit increases by $40 billion). This would satisfy the requirement stated above that net income be increased by $150 billion to $200 billion.

The commission's recommendations decreased the average 75-year OASDI deficit of 1.82 percent of taxable payroll to 0.58 percent, thus eliminating only about two-thirds of that deficit. No agreement could be reached by the commission on how to eliminate the remaining deficit. Some members favored a higher retirement age, some preferred higher taxes, and some preferred reduced benefits.

The commission virtually ignored the HI deficit of 5.21 percent of taxable payroll, which is almost three times the OASDI deficit of 1.82 percent. The commission also completely ignored the Supplementary Medical Insurance (SMI) part of Medicare, 25 percent of which is financed by premiums paid by participants and 75 percent of which is financed by general revenue. The total cost of SMI is now the equivalent of about 1 percent of taxable payroll and is projected to rise to some 5 percent during the lifetime of today's youth.

There is nothing mysterious about Medicare: it is a life annuity, paid in kind rather than cash, primarily to social security beneficiaries age 65 and older. Almost one-fifth of the taxpayer's FICA (Federal Insurance Contribution Act) tax is now used to finance the

HI portion of Medicare. Medicare is a part of social security; ignoring Medicare's problems will not make them disappear.

Although the commission did not address the financial problems of the HI program, and in spite of that program's imminent financial difficulties, the commission recommended that the OASDI trust fund be authorized to continue borrowing from the HI trust funds during the 1983–87 period.

It is apparent that the commission's recommendations did not even come close to resolving social security's financial problems—except those of the OASDI program through 1989.[2] To resolve longer-range financial problems the tax rate would have to rise considerably above its scheduled level of 7.65 percent for 1990. Under the intermediate assumptions adopted by the commission, the rate would have to increase to about 14 percent early in the next century, within the working lifetime of today's young taxpayers. And under less optimistic assumptions, the tax rate would have to increase to about 20 percent—a combined employer-employee tax rate of 40 percent. This is almost three times the ultimate scheduled rate of 7.65 percent.[3] This tax increase is in addition to the cost of the Supplemental Medical Insurance (SMI) part of Medicare mentioned above.

There are, of course, alternatives to these onerous tax rates. The retirement age could be increased to about 70 for persons under 35, or benefits for future retirees could be reduced somewhat, or the entire system could be restructured to reflect the changing social and economic environment. But the commission could not consider changes of this type without acknowledging a longer range problem—and this it failed to do.

The commission considered it a major achievement that it got the

---

[2]Under less optimistic (but not inconceivable) economic assumptions, the commission's recommendations would fail to sustain the OASDI system through the 1980s, and further remedial action would be required.

[3]For long-range planning purposes, it appears prudent to rely upon demographic and economic assumptions that are less optimistic than those adopted by the commission. For example, the commission's intermediate assumptions were that the fertility rate will eventually rise about 12 percent above its present level. By assuming higher-than-realistic fertility rates, the commission was assuming lower-than-realistic future costs. It is wishful thinking to assume that fertility rates will rise above current levels and to make future promises of benefits on that basis. All indications—including the latest population projections by the Bureau of the Census—are that fertility rates will remain at their present levels or else decline.

minority of the commissioners representing those who favor the status quo to admit the existence of a relatively minor financial problem during the period 1983–89. It should not be surprising, therefore, that the commission was unable to acknowledge the existence of major financial and structural problems that may not become critical for another 10 years.

Appropriateness of the Recommendations

It is tempting to criticize the commission for not recommending the "correct solution" to social security's problems; however, there is no such correct solution. The "proper design" for social security

---

Figure 1

PROJECTED EXPENDITURES AND LEGISLATED INCOME UNDER SOCIAL SECURITY (% OF TAXABLE PAYROLL)

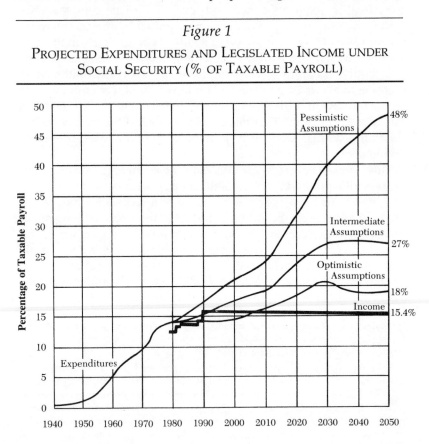

SOURCE: Derived from data in A. Haeworth Robertson, *The Coming Revolution in Social Security* (McLean, Va.: Security Press, 1981), chap. 7.

depends upon one's values and beliefs about social ethics. Unanimity among diverse interest groups should not be expected. Nevertheless, the following limited commentary may be of value in assessing the recommendations offered by the commission.

For 47 years the public has thought social security's benefits inviolable. People believed that if the government promised a certain type and level of benefit, it would be paid. People were told that by paying "contributions" to social security, they were acquiring "earned rights" to certain benefits. In fact, there has been a steady expansion of benefits, and people have generally received even more than promised. As recently as December 7, 1979, the Advisory Council on Social Security had the temerity to declare: "After reviewing the evidence, the Council is unanimously convinced that all current and future Social Security beneficiaries can count on receiving all benefits to which they are entitled."[4]

It should be evident that it is no longer true that benefits once promised will certainly be paid. Witness the cuts in student benefits and minimum benefits that occurred in 1981. Witness the commission's recommendation to defer the cost-of-living adjustment for six months. Witness the recommendation to indirectly decrease benefits now being paid to people with income excluding social security of $20,000 or more for a single taxpayer or of $25,000 or more for joint-return taxpayers by taxing half their social security benefits.[5]

One disturbing aspect of this selective reduction of benefits by taxing them is the implication that if a person saves successfully for retirement, he will be rewarded by a reduction in the benefits he presumably counted upon in making his retirement plans. If this means-test philosophy is carried to its logical conclusion, the government will effectively discourage the disclosure of other income. Such a government-induced change in citizen behavior would be extremely damaging to the character of our nation.

Furthermore, by reneging on its promised benefits the government will have damaged its image and that of social security. This

---

[4]Social Security Administration, Department of Health, Education, and Welfare, Advisory Council on Social Security, *Social Security Financing and Benefits: Reports of the 1979 Advisory Council on Social Security* (Washington: Government Printing Office, 1979), p. 18.

[5]At the outset, this effective reduction of benefits would apply to only about 10 percent of OASDI beneficiaries. But since the reduction is not indexed, inflation would eventually cause it to apply to virtually all beneficiaries.

loss of credibility will make it difficult to convince younger taxpayers that social security will honor its promise to pay benefits to them some 30 to 50 years hence. Without such a conviction, taxpayers will be very reluctant to pay the high taxes necessary to support the system in the years ahead.

Higher Retirement Ages

The commission's recommendations made no mention of the inevitable increase in normal retirement age (from 65 to at least 70) for persons now younger than about 35 or 40. This increase will be absolutely necessary to provide the nation with an appropriate-sized work force, not just to resolve social security's financial problems. When today's youngsters retire at age 70 in the next century, they will have more years left to live than their forebears who retired at 65. A higher retirement age is *not* a benefit cut; it is a natural consequence of increasing life-spans and improved health. The only tenable way for today's youngsters to retire in their early sixties would be for them to have the same, shorter life-spans as their forebears—not a very attractive alternative.

The commission not only failed to propose higher retirement ages, it indicated that for people to defer their retirement beyond 65 would not provide any substantial relief to social security. This conclusion stemmed from the commission's proposal to increase the delayed retirement credit for individuals between 65 and 70 from 3 to 8 percent per year. This is an unrealistic proposal, directly contrary to the need for increasing the retirement age and decreasing the retirement benefits for future retirees.

Increased Taxes

The commission's proposals to increase the social security system's net income by $169 billion during the period 1983–89 were made up of both benefit decreases and tax increases, with emphasis on the latter. In the face of an immediate fiscal crisis, this emphasis on tax increases may be preferable to an emphasis on benefit decreases. But the system's current financial problems did not arise overnight—they have been in the making since the mid-1970s. Contingency plans could have been made that would have permitted a more even balance between tax increases and benefit decreases.

Parenthetically, we have the same opportunity *now* to make plans for accommodating the impending Medicare deficits and to restructure the OASDI program to reflect demographic shifts, the changing role of women in the work force, and so on. Ten years from now, as we frantically search for solutions to this "surprise crisis," we will decry the lack of time to develop well-designed solutions and will once more resort to hastily designed compromises.

Unfortunately, waiting until the last possible moment to resolve the system's financial problems virtually forces the government to use general revenue, and a large part of the commission's recommended tax increase was slated to come from general revenue, particularly in 1983 and 1984. As nearly everyone knows, the nation's budget has a deficit, and there is no general revenue available to use for social security. Relying on general revenue to pay benefits is thus tantamount to borrowing—not a very sound basis on which to operate a social insurance system.

The extent of the commission's proposed use of general revenue may not be obvious at first glance because it was to be done in the following rather indirect manner. First, the increase in the employee social security tax for 1984 (from 6.7 to 7.0 percent) was to be returned to the employee as a tax credit or cash refund, thus reducing general revenue by the same amount as the tax increase. Second, one-half of the total, increased self-employment social security tax was to be deductible as a business expense, thus reducing general revenue by a substantial portion of the tax increase.[6] And third, the lump-sum reimbursement to the old-age trust funds for military-wage credits was to come from general revenue.[7]

[6]Although this procedure places the high-income self-employed in the same after-tax position as did the former procedure, it places a much larger tax burden on the lower-income self-employed.

[7]This is the ultimate example of how waiting until the last minute to resolve social security's financial problems can evoke desperate, even ludicrous, "solutions" that have no substance whatsoever.

Under social security, gratuitous military-service credits are granted in some cases without the recipient's having paid social security taxes. To prevent a loss to the trust funds, the former procedure was to use general revenue to reimburse those funds the amount of the benefits arising from these credits at the time the benefits were actually paid. The recommendation of the commission sought to change this procedure, requiring general-revenue reimbursement to the trust fund in *advance* of the disbursement of benefits. This advance funding of military credits could then be used to meet the current shortfall in the trust funds and permit the continued payment of benefits to other recipients.

Careful analysis reveals this to be an artful machination of the government to give the public a false sense of security without taking any substantive action. The actual procedure is to take funds from nonexistent general revenue (i.e., raise the national debt by borrowing from the taxpayers) and to pay amounts to social security that

A more subtle introduction of general revenue into the system arises from the addition of newly hired federal employees to social security. Putting all federal employees into the system was expected to bring a financial gain because more social security tax money is paid by federal employees than is paid out in benefits to them. But the ultimate source of taxes paid into the system by federal employees is general revenue. Therefore, including federal employees in social security simply causes a shift from direct payroll tax financing to indirect general-revenue financing.

Although it is not widely known, general revenue is already used to finance three-fourths of the cost of the SMI portion (Part B) of Medicare. In 1982 the total cost of SMI was about $17 billion, or the equivalent of about 1 percent of taxable payroll. With the total cost of SMI projected to rise to 5 percent of payroll, general-revenue SMI financing will therefore eventually amount to nearly 4 percent of payroll. This is twice what the entire social security program cost—a combined employer-employee tax of 2 percent—when it was originally adopted.

Universal Mandatory Coverage

As desirable as universal mandatory participation in social security might be from several viewpoints, it seems grossly unfair to ban the withdrawal of state and local government employers from the system. These employers (and their employees) voluntarily joined social security with the understanding that they could withdraw in the future. A unilateral change in this participation agreement seems highly undesirable, if not illegal. State and local governments should at least have a grace period in which to make a final irrevocable decision as to whether they want to withdraw from social security or continue to participate in it.

Mandatory coverage of newly hired federal employees may likewise be desirable in some respects, but it is doubtful that it would save the nation any money—although some advocates of mandatory coverage suggest it would. It is likely that new hirees would receive the same total benefits from social security and a revised Civil Service retirement system as they now receive from their

---

are not due for many years to come so that those funds can be used to pay current beneficiaries. The net result was a $20 billion increase in the national debt in 1983 so that $20 billion could be added to social security trust funds to stave off insolvency for a few more months.

present system. If so, the total cost of retirement benefits for federal employees would not be reduced; it would simply be rearranged.

Mandatory universal coverage would be reasonable if social security provided only a minimum floor of protection. But social security is not a minimum floor of protection; it provides an array of benefits far beyond those that everyone would agree is a socially desirable minimum. Accordingly, it does not seem reasonable to impose the existing program on everyone whether they need it or not. If social security were reformed to provide a level and array of benefits that most people could agree were socially desirable, then mandatory universal coverage would be in order.

Problem Is Not Just Financial

In defining the size and scope of the social security problem, the commission gave practically no attention to the strong likelihood that the long-range problem is primarily a *design* problem and not just a financial problem. The social and economic environment will be considerably different 30 to 50 years from now, when the children of the post–World War II baby boom approach retirement. The role of women in society and the workplace has changed and will continue to evolve. It is entirely reasonable, therefore, to give serious consideration to a completely new type of social insurance system for the younger segment of our population, even if we continue the present system for the older segment.

What did the commission have to say on this subject? During the final days of its meetings, the commission acknowledged that it was committed to the basic structure of the existing social security system and contemplated no recommendations for major change. Several members of the commission noted that the social and economic environment had changed more rapidly than had social security and that a reexamination of the system's basic structure was therefore in order. They stated, however, that the pressures imposed by the size of the financial problems had diverted their attention from such a comprehensive study. This statement seems absurd for two reasons.

First, the commission was appointed in December 1981, when the financial problems were well known and well documented, and thus had more than adequate time for a thorough study. Second, the inappropriate design of social security is a significant factor in causing the long-range financial problems and in causing doubt about the fairness, and thus the long-term viability, of the system.

Approximately 80 percent of the nonretired population is younger than 45. It is this large group that is questioning whether social security will still be around at retirement. The program's future depends precisely upon whether or not today's youth will support it, and this depends in turn upon whether it suits their needs and whether they believe it to be fair.

Restoration of Public Confidence

The commission attempted to design recommendations for change in social security that would simultaneously resolve the system's financial problems and restore the public's confidence in the long-range viability of the system. This effort to restore public confidence is of paramount importance in view of findings by respected polls that there is now little confidence, especially among young people, that the program will continue to operate in the long-range future.[8] Confidence in the continuation of social security is essential, of course, if the taxpayers are to keep supporting the system.

Although much of the commission's work may be commendable in view of the circumstances, adopting the commission's recommendations clearly cannot resolve very many of social security's financial problems. *If the public is misled into believing that the financial problems of social security have been resolved, there will be a very harsh day of reckoning in the not-too-distant future.* If public confidence in the system and in the government itself erodes any further, the stability of the nation may be in danger.

If Congress does not do a better job than the commission at recognizing social security's significant future financial problems, it may soon be too late to develop rational solutions, since an atmosphere of crisis seldom yields satisfactory results—as shown by the present situation. If Congress tries to solve future financial problems without resolving future *design* problems, and thus without gaining greater public support, its efforts will be in vain. Much bolder action will be required by Congress than was recommended by the commission if social security's problems are truly to be resolved and if the public's steadily eroding confidence is to be restored. And we need to pay more serious attention to the obvious problems that lie ahead. Realism may be painful, but it is not nearly as fatal as unjustified optimism.

[8]Louis Harris and Associates, Inc., *1979 Study of American Attitudes toward Pensions and Retirement* (New York: Johnson and Higgins, 1979), p. 94.

EDITOR'S COMMENT

The Congress and the president immediately embraced the commission's recommendations. Because of widespread fear in Washington that any attempted alteration of any single element in the package would make the whole compromise unravel, the commission's proposals were enacted almost without change.

One significant modification was made, however, in the recommendation to subject social security benefits to the federal income tax. Social security benefits were previously excluded from income when calculating federal income tax liability. As noted by Robertson, the commission recommended that half of a person's social security benefits be included in taxable income for single persons with incomes over $20,000 and for married persons with joint incomes over $25,000.[1] This proposal, however, created the enormous threshold problem discussed by economist Paul Craig Roberts below. A married couple earning $24,999 would have the entire tax burden on half their social security benefits triggered merely by earning an extra dollar, resulting in perhaps thousands of dollars in increased tax liability. This would create a ludicrous marginal tax rate for many taxpayers, possibly as high as 100,000 percent.

The final legislation therefore provided for income thresholds of $25,000 for single persons and $32,000 for couples.[2] Moreover, social security benefits were included in taxable income only up to one-half the difference between income and the threshold, until one-half the total benefits were so included. This phases in the taxation of benefits as income rises more and more above the threshold, rather than triggering the whole tax burden upon reaching the threshold. But as Roberts suggests below, these changes merely transformed a ludicrous provision into a major disaster, for marginal tax rates still remain incredibly high for income ranges above

[1]For these purposes, "income" is defined as adjusted gross income from all sources other than social security.

[2]The legislation provided that interest from tax-exempt bonds be included in the definition of this income.

49

the threshold. An important economic effect of these high marginal rates is to discourage saving for supplementary retirement income.

Congress also added one major element to the commission's package of proposals: a provision raising the retirement age for full benefits from 65 to 67. Starting in 2000, the normal retirement age will be delayed for two months each year for people reaching age 62 in that year, until the normal age is delayed to 66 in 2005. In 2017, the age will be delayed for two months a year again until it reaches 67 in 2022. Early retirement will still be available at 62, but at a greater reduction in benefits.

The story of the 1983 social security rescue legislation holds at least three important lessons. First, it illustrates the extreme political difficulty of attacking social security benefits head on. The administration's 1981 benefit reduction proposals were prudent and rational, aimed at rescuing the program from an officially recognized, impending financial collapse, and they were issued by a popular president just elected by a landslide. Yet they were immediately hooted out of town on a 96-0 vote by the most conservative Senate since the days of Calvin Coolidge, controlled by the president's own party.

Second, the story illustrates the success of the old guard strategy of delaying any action on social security's impending financial collapse for as long as possible. By the time the commission and the Congress acted in early 1983, the collapse was only a few months away. Addressing the problem with benefit reductions at that point would have meant sudden losses of income to current retirees, income they could well have already spent through credit obligations, mortgage burdens, or fixed rental demands. Such immediate, peremptory cuts were not even remotely within the realm of political plausibility. Consequently, the program's short-term financial crisis had to be solved, as it was, predominantly by providing increased revenues. Social security's old guard establishment is now pursuing the same strategy for HI benefits in the short run and for the entire program's continuing financial problems in the long run.

Finally, the story reveals the political hyprocrisy of the old guard establishment's professed devotion to the elderly. After allies of the old guard campaigned all of fall 1982 on the theme that Reagan would slash benefits to the elderly right after the election, it was the old guard and its allies, through Commissioners Moynihan and Ball, that advanced the one element of the rescue legislation that did cut existing benefits for today's elderly—the taxation of benefits.

The 1983 rescue legislation as passed managed to hurt just about everyone:

- the elderly saw their benefits cut;
- workers saw their taxes raised substantially;
- young people saw their future, promised returns under the program cut to almost nothing;
- virtually every worker in the economy was corralled into the insatiable program against his will;
- the principle of self-financing was dashed through massive infusions of general revenue into the system.

Yet this legislation was passed over alternative, more fundamental reform because it was supposed to be more salable politically. Clearly, the legislation did just about everything that could be done within the current framework of the system.

Right after the 1983 rescue legislation was passed, the old guard establishment again began announcing to the nation that social security would now be financially sound well into the next century. But the truth is that deep financial problems still threatened the program in both the short and long terms.

In the short run, the program remained vulnerable to the cycles of inflation and recession that have dominated the American economy for the last 20 years. Inflation causes social security benefits to rise faster than expected because benefits are indexed to increase with inflation. But recession causes wage and employment growth, and hence projected payroll tax revenues, to fall. Without a large cushion of saved assets in the social security trust funds, back-to-back sharp inflation and steep recession can easily throw the entire program into bankruptcy. It was the inflation and legislatively increased benefits of the early 1970s followed by the 1974–75 recession that resulted in the need for the 1977 social security rescue legislation. And it was the inflation of the late 1970s followed by the recession of 1979–82 that caused the most recent social security financial collapse.

Recent studies indicate that the social security trust funds need assets equal to 85 to 145 percent of one year's expenditures to survive a serious recession or close back-to-back recessions as were experienced from 1973 to 1982.[3] Yet the SSA's own latest projections under the "intermediate" Alternative IIB projections show that, even excluding the financially troubled HI portion of the program, the 85 percent level would not be reached until 1992, and 145 percent would not be reached until 1996.[4] Under "pessimistic" Alternative III assumptions, 85 percent would not be reached until 1999, and 145 percent would not be reached until 2005.[5]

Consequently, despite all the pain and suffering imposed by the 1983 legislation, the program is still vulnerable to yet another financial collapse due to an economic downturn consistent with long-established trends in the U.S. economy. Indeed, if the economic slowdown in late 1984 had turned into a serious recession, as many feared, then social security would soon be facing another financial crisis. The simple continuation of the economic performance of the 1970s would have produced another social security crisis just a few years after the 1983 legislation.

This vulnerability remains today and will continue at least until the trust fund levels indicated above are reached. If those who are warning about an economic calamity on the horizon due to current large budget deficits prove correct, then social security can also be expected to face another financial collapse soon.

The SSA's own deputy chief actuary responsible for short-term projections acknowledged the continuing danger faced by the program in a briefing memorandum distributed within the administration soon after passage of the 1983 legislation. He wrote:

> If actual growth is more rapid in 1983, but then restricted by another recession within the next few years, the trust funds would be in a worse financial position than indicated under [pessimistic assumptions]. . . . Depletion of the . . . trust funds would be very likely under these conditions and could conceivably occur within a few years from now.[6]

---

[3]Alicia H. Munnell and Lynn E. Blais, "Do We Want Large Social Security Surpluses?" *New England Economic Review* (September/October 1984).

[4]*1984 OASDI Report.*

[5]Ibid.

[6]Richard S. Foster, memorandum, "Short-Range Financial Status of the Social Security Program Under the Social Security Amendments of 1983," April 6, 1983, p. 3.

The *1984 OASDI Report* also repeatedly warned of the program's vulnerability to a sharp recession at least until 1987.[7]

Moreover, as usual the problem is worse than the SSA expects. The 1983 legislation relied on large payroll tax increases now scheduled for 1988 and 1990 to move the program eventually out of the range of short-term vulnerability to inflation and recession. But these tax increases will harm the economy and lower employment, leading to less new revenue than expected. Other elements in the legislation will also fail to meet expectations based on the official static estimates. The taxation of benefits will cause many of the elderly potentially subject to the tax to shelter their incomes to fall below the taxation-triggering income thresholds. The increase in the self-employment tax will result in fewer self-employed workers, earning less income than expected. These and other possible shortfalls will extend social security's short-term vulnerability to weak economic performance.

Most important of all, this analysis, as noted, excludes the HI portion of social security, which will be unable to pay promised benefits sometime in the next decade under the SSA's own projections, despite recent improvement in the short-term outlook for HI.[8] If OASDI funds could be used to pay HI benefits when necessary, then HI would eventually consume much of the surpluses from the rest of the program, possibly leaving social security as a whole indefinitely vulnerable to short-term collapse due to the effects of inflation and recession. With economic performance similar to that in the 1970s, adding in HI would be enough for social security as a whole to collapse again near the end of the next decade, just when the program is supposed to be accumulating large surpluses to aid in the payment of benefits when the baby-boom generation retires. The latest SSA projections in fact show that under Alternative III assumptions, which overall assume better economic performance than in the 1970s, absorbing the HI deficits into the rest of the program again leaves all of social security unable to pay promised benefits in the late 1990s.[9]

This analysis reveals the short-term vulnerabilities of social security, but another collapse soon is not inevitable. With those born during the postwar baby boom now swelling the taxpaying work

[7] *1984 OASDI Report.*
[8] *1985 Annual Report of the Board of Trustees of the Hospital Insurance Program.*
[9] *1985 OASDI Report; 1985 HI Report.*

force in earnest, plus the still further tax increases scheduled in the coming years, the near future could naturally be expected to be one of the brightest financial periods of the program. Federal pricing controls recently imposed on medical services under Medicare are also substantially reducing projected HI expenditures and deficits.[10] Most importantly, however, the Reagan economic boom is profoundly enhancing the short-term financial prospects for social security. As long as this boom continues without serious inflation or recession, social security will not experience another financial crisis in the short term. Indeed, if this boom somehow continues uninterrupted throughout the 1990s, long-projected substantial annual surpluses in social security will surely appear, even after absorbing the HI deficits. The short-term salvation of social security would then be another major accomplishment credited to the Reagan recovery.

Those attuned to the financial vulnerabilities of social security should not be surprised by this possible development. The short-term surpluses would create new opportunities for reform, such as eliminating the scheduled 1988 and 1990 tax increases and allowing workers to opt out of portions of the program directly. Market-oriented policymakers do need to start taking these possible surpluses into account in planning reforms for the program.

But reappearance of the inflation and recession cycles that have been common in recent experience would again eventually produce another short-term social security collapse. And there is little reason at this point to believe that the Reagan administration's economic policies have permanently eliminated such cycles. In any event, the primary variable determining how social security will fare over the short term is the performance of the economy.

Even the development of substantial social security surpluses

[10]Under the Prospective Payment System for Medicare, the federal government sets the fees it will pay hospitals for various medical services and prohibits hospitals from charging patients or their insurance companies more than that. This system provides strong incentives for hospitals to shortchange medical services for Medicare patients, likely leading eventually to a marked deterioration in service quality. The system will tend to operate like price controls over the long run, leading to a rationing of medical care and even further quality deterioration. It is not an acceptable, permanent means of reducing Medicare costs. For further discussion, see Peter J. Ferrara, "Medicare Solution: Health Bank IRAs," *Journal of the Institute for Socioeconomic Studies* (Spring 1985). Moreover, the savings resulting from this system may prove to be a one-shot affair, with long-term trends of above-normal inflation in medical costs resuming after a few years.

over the short term, however, will not alter the long-term outlook for the program because the SSA is already assuming that such surpluses will occur and is relying on them to finance future benefits. The latest available SSA projections under Alternative IIB assumptions show that social security, excluding HI, would begin running large annual surpluses starting at the end of this decade and lasting until around 2015, leading to the accumulation of a large trust fund.[11] By 2020, however, large annual deficits appear, continuing indefinitely and exhausting the trust fund by 2049.[12] By 2050, social security expenditures, excluding HI, would be running 8 percent higher than revenues each year.[13] It is clearly only the large surpluses accumulated earlier in the projection period that would allow benefits to continue to be paid even this long.

Adding HI to the analysis, the long-run financial problems for the program become much more serious. Assuming assets from any of the program's trust funds could be used to pay any of the program's benefits when necessary, the entire, combined social security program would become unable to pay promised benefits by the time those entering the work force today retired.[14] By 2035, social security expenditures would be running almost 50 percent greater than revenues each year.[15] Over the entire 75-year projection period, the program as a whole would run a cumulative deficit 150 percent as large as the total amount raised in new revenue or cut in benefits over the same period by the 1983 rescue legislation.[16]

This long-term problem is primarily a result of demographics. During the baby-boom years following World War II, fertility rates (lifetime births per woman) were especially high, producing an especially large generation. But the baby boom has been followed by almost 30 years now of fertility rapidly declining and eventually stabilizing at much lower rates, resulting in a relatively small generation following the older baby-boom population. The fertility rate fell from about 3.7 in 1957 to about 1.8 in the late 1970s, less than half the 1957 rate.[17]

---

[11] *1984 OASDI Report.*
[12] Ibid.
[13] Ibid.
[14] Calculated from the *1985 OASDI Report* and *1985 HI Report.*
[15] *1985 OASDI Report,* app. E.
[16] Ibid.
[17] *1985 OASDI Report.*

This development is a disaster for a pay-as-you-go system like social security, where benefits for each generation of retirees are financed primarily by the taxes of the following generation of workers. When the especially large baby-boom generation, which is now in the work force and consequently enhancing social security financing, reaches retirement, it will naturally place an especially heavy benefit burden on the system. But at the same time, the relatively small working generation behind it will be generating an especially weak flow of revenues. The result is a great potential for a disastrous financial collapse.

Indeed, the long-term financial prospects for the program may be much worse than indicated by the projections discussed above because the underlying Alternative IIB assumptions may be over-optimistic in many crucial aspects. The most important of these is probably mortality assumptions. The Alternative IIB assumptions in fact assume a slowdown in the rate of increase in life expectancy that we have been experiencing for the last 40 years.[18] But if future retirees live longer than now projected, they will draw more benefits from the program, adding to its financial difficulties. We are even now entering a new technological age with the potential for dramatic medical breakthroughs. Over the next 75 years, major discoveries could extend life expectancy well beyond what we might now dare guess. Yet, if the baby-boom generation were to live on average only 10 years or so more than now projected, the financial impact on social security would be overwhelming. Current social security projections fail to account for this potential adequately, and the assumed Alternative IIB life expectancies could be easily surpassed. Longer life expectancies in fact hold the potential for becoming the new chief source of intractable financial problems for social security.

The Alternative IIB assumptions also leave little room for periods of weak economic performance over the next 75 years. For example, inflation and unemployment are assumed to stabilize at 4 percent and 6 percent respectively over the next few years and to remain at those levels each year until 2060.[19] The assumed performance of other economic variables is similar. These assumptions may be reasonable for individual, good economic years, but given the background of our current economic institutions and policies, they are

[18]Ibid.
[19]Ibid.

not likely to be correct as averages over 70 years, when periodic bouts of inflation and recession may still be expected. These assumptions in effect assume that there will not be another major recession or serious stretch of inflation for the next 75 years.

The Alternative IIB assumptions also assume favorable fertility trends. The fertility rate is assumed to increase substantially and permanently from current levels.[20] Yet the downward trend in fertility rates has a 200-year history, falling from 7.04 in 1800 to 1.76 today.[21] There are powerful social, economic, and technological trends behind this long-term decline that, if anything, portend further declines. Many Western European countries have significantly lower rates than the United States, including West Germany with a rate of 1.4. Moreover, it took the back-to-back cataclysms of the Great Depression and World War II to produce the relatively brief fertility increase of the postwar baby boom. The lower the fertility rates are, of course, the fewer workers there will be to finance the accrued benefit obligations under social security's pay-as-you-go system, worsening the financial outlook for the program.

More realistic long-term projections of social security financing may, therefore, be provided by the supposedly pessimistic Alternative III assumptions. Inflation here, for example, is assumed to stabilize permanently at 5.0 percent, and unemployment at 7.0 percent.[22] Both fertility and life expectancy are projected to follow longstanding trends more closely.[23] In the past, as we have noted, reality has generally most closely followed the Alternative III projections.

Under Alternative III projections, the entire, combined social security program would be unable to pay full benefits before the end of the next decade.[24] By 2035, social security expenditures under these projections would be two-and-one-third times as large as revenues each year.[25] The cumulative deficit over the 75-year projection period would be more than 4.5 times as large as the financial gap addressed by the 1983 legislation.[26]

[20]Ibid.

[21]See Ferrara, *The Inherent Contradiction,* table 33; *1985 OASDI Report.*

[22]*1985 OASDI Report.*

[23]Ibid.

[24]Ibid.; *1985 HI Report.*

[25]*1985 OASDI Report,* app. E.

[26]Ibid.

In order to pay the benefits promised to those entering the work force today, under Alternative III assumptions the combined employer-employee social security payroll tax rate would have to be raised to 37.5 percent, compared with 14.1 percent today.[27] This would mean a total annual social security tax, split between employer and employee, of $7,500 for a worker making $20,000.

The Alternative III assumptions are far from outlandish; they could quite easily occur in reality, and the SSA itself in effect admits that they are possible. It would certainly be the most prudent to make both public policy and individual plans based on such assumptions. On this basis, social security may still be expected to face financial disaster over the long term, and fundamental reform should be adopted now to avoid it. Until such reform is adopted, the best advice for today's young workers remains: Do not make your future financial plans on the expectation of receiving currently promised social security benefits.

In the paper below, Paul Craig Roberts, former assistant secretary of the treasury for economic policy, discusses some of the structural factors in the social security system contributing to its financial difficulties.

[27]Ibid.

III. Social Security: Myths and Realities

Paul Craig Roberts

Introduction

Shortly after the 1981 inauguration, the Reagan administration faced a crisis in social security, despite the 1977 amendments that President Carter promised would make social security sound through the turn of the century. The largest of the system's three programs, Old-Age and Survivors Insurance (OASI), was likely to run out of money during Reagan's term of office unless economic growth proved robust. The long-run prospects of the combined system (OASDHI) included large perpetual deficits and were even more dismal.

The Treasury recognized that social security was an unfunded system of taxes and transfer payments that was unaffordable at the current rate of growth in benefits, and the Office of Economic Policy developed a plan for putting the program on a realistic basis. However, other parts of the government had different goals, and the opportunity was lost. The Office of Management and Budget concentrated on short-run budget savings in order to lower current federal budget deficits. The Department of Health and Human Services was preoccupied with its effort to rid the system of various welfare elements. Robert Myers and the Social Security Administration were determined to keep social security on an expanding course as the main source of retirement income. As a result, the Treasury was frustrated in its effort to focus attention on the realities of the system. Instead, the myth that social security is an affordable pension system was perpetuated, and a new myth was born—that the government will deal responsibly with the long-run social security problem.

The author holds the William E. Simon Chair in Political Economy at the Center for Strategic and International Studies, Georgetown University. This paper is drawn from his work *The Supply-Side Revolution: An Insider's Account of Policymaking in Washington* (Cambridge, Mass.: Harvard University Press, 1984).

The Source of the Problem: The 1972 Social Security Amendments

There are two major areas of social security that involve indexes. The one most people think of is the annual cost-of-living adjustment (COLA), which occurred each July 1 until the 1983 social security amendments moved the date to January 1. This adjustment increases benefits going to current retirees by the amount of inflation each year, as measured by the consumer price index. Thus, whatever benefit the worker receives upon first retiring is preserved in real terms and protected from inflation. The cost-of-living adjustment is often blamed for the deficits in the social security accounts and the overall federal budget, but it is not the real culprit.

The other area of indexing is the real source of the system's long-run troubles. When a worker retires, the amount of his first social security check, or initial benefit, is computed by a formula that involves wage indexes. These indexes cause the real value of each retiring generation's initial benefits to rise over time. The COLA merely preserves the real value of these benefits over the individual's retirement period. It is the buildup of the real levels of the *initial* benefits, generation after generation, that is leading to the system's ruin.

Prior to the 1972 amendments, Congress had raised social security benefits over the years on an ad hoc basis. However, a 15 percent benefit increase in 1970, a 10 percent increase in 1971, and a 20 percent increase in 1972 represented quantum jumps in benefit levels. These were reinforced by the 1972 social security amendments, which were supposed to preserve these increases with automatic inflation adjustments each year, beginning in 1975.

Unfortunately, the 1972 amendments contained a major formula error, which has become known as the "double indexing" or "decoupling" problem. It resulted in sharp increases in benefits for new retirees just entering the system and caused benefits to rise faster than wages. An average worker retiring in 1969 could expect to receive a tax-exempt social security benefit equal to 31 percent of his last working year's gross income. By 1972, ad hoc increases by the Congress had raised this so-called replacement rate to 38 percent. As a result of the automatic adjustments in the 1972 amendments it rose to 41 percent in 1974, 44 percent in 1976, and 55 percent in 1981.[1]

---

[1] These historical replacement rates are taken from unpublished tables prepared by the Office of the Actuary, Social Security Administration, August 1981.

The source of the problem was fairly straightforward. The initial social security benefit a worker received upon retiring was computed in two steps. First, the worker's gross wages from 1951 until the date of retirement were added up and averaged over the number of months worked to determine an average monthly wage. This wage, split into several "brackets," was then multiplied by an array of percentages called the "marginal benefit rates," which were set by law. The product was the worker's initial social security check. For example, if the benefit rates averaged 0.40, then the worker's first retirement check would equal 40 percent of his average wage. The 1972 amendments provided for the annual adjustment of the marginal benefit rates for each year's population of retirees by the amount of inflation over the year. For example, if inflation had been 10 percent and the old benefit rates had averaged 0.40, the new benefit rates would average 0.44. Unfortunately, complete adjustment of the benefit rates for inflation overadjusted benefits. Over time, wages tend to rise with inflation. While wages earned in the distant past were, of course, not adjusted for recent inflation, wages earned in the years immediately preceding retirement would have been largely adjusted for inflation. Consequently, one part of the benefit computation, the average monthly wage, was already partially adjusted for inflation by the marketplace.

The correct way to increase the product of two numbers by, for example, 10 percent is to increase one or the other number by 10 percent, but not both. By adjusting the benefit rates completely when the average monthly wage had already received partial adjustment for inflation, the formula made the resulting benefits grow faster than inflation.

The Perpetuation of the Problem: The 1977 Amendments

The 1977 amendments stopped the initial benefits from rising faster than wages but allowed the initial benefits of each retiring generation to keep pace with real wages over time. This was not enough of a reduction in benefit growth to deal with the long-run problem, leaving the system on a path of expansion that will carry outlays significantly beyond currently scheduled tax rates. Under the economic assumptions (Alternative IIB) in the 1982 trustees report, OASDI benefits were scheduled to rise as a percentage of payroll from 10–12 percent near term to 17–18 percent long term. This compared with a scheduled OASDI tax rate of 12.4 percent of payroll after 1990. After a few years of surplus, beginning in the

61

1990s, a deficit appeared shortly after 2010, widening to a permanent gap of roughly 5 percent of payroll between outlays and receipts in OASDI after 2025.

Adding in Hospital Insurance (HI) makes the deficit worse. The combined OASDHI system's outlays were projected to rise as a percentage of payroll from 15 percent near term to 27–30 percent long term. This compared with the scheduled OASDHI tax rate of 15.3 percent after 1990. A deficit appeared shortly after 1995, widening to a permanent gap of roughly 12–15 percent of payroll between outlays and receipts in OASDHI after 2025. This translated into an annual deficit in excess of $300 billion by 2025 and in excess of $600 billion by 2060, measured in real 1983 dollars.[2]

The source of the long-run deficits is twofold. First there are the demographics. As the population grows more slowly over time, the population ages and there are more retirees per worker. Second, the indexing formula allows initial benefits to grow indefinitely in real terms at the same pace as wages. With real benefits per retiree rising along with real wages, but with the number of retirees rising faster than the number of wage earners, the cost of the system must rise as a percentage of payroll. Consequently, either payroll tax rates must rise sharply, taking more out of each dollar of wages, or the growth of real benefit levels must be reexamined.

The social security system is in crisis because it is scheduled to pay ever-rising real benefits to successive generations. One way to deal with the problem is to reduce the scheduled rise in benefits. A switch from wage indexing (under which real benefits per retiree would triple in three generations) to price indexing (under which real benefits per retiree would roughly double) would essentially eliminate the long-run OASDI problem.

Price indexing was recommended in the 1976 Hsiao report.[3] The Finance Committee under Senator Long was receptive to the proposal. The Treasury, led by Secretary William E. Simon, was also eager to take the more responsible course. However, there was an election approaching. President Ford, at the apparent urging of his

[2]*1982 Annual Report of the Board of Trustees of the Federal Old-Age and Survivors Insurance and Disability Insurance Trust Funds* (Washington: Government Printing Office, April 1, 1982), table 27, p. 64.

[3]See William C. Hsiao, "An Optimal Indexing Method for Social Security," in *Financing Social Security*, ed. Colin D. Campbell (Washington: American Enterprise Institute, 1979), pp. 19–40.

political advisors and with the apparent blessing of his chairman of economic advisers, Alan Greenspan, wished to appear more generous. Ford opted for the much more expensive wage-indexing procedure. This single mistake added well over $2 *trillion* in unfunded liability in present-value terms to the system's long-run deficit. It accounts for *more than 100 percent* of OASDI's deficit.

The Misleading Concept of Actuarial Balance

The long-run problem is hidden by a misleading statistic. It is called the "actuarial balance" of the OASDI system. (The HI portion is generally excluded.) The Social Security Administration (SSA) generally reports on the condition of the OASDI trust funds over a 75-year future planning period. It says the system is in "actuarial balance" if the average income of the system measured as a percentage of payroll equals the average cost of benefits measured as a percentage of payroll over 75 years. In 1982, the OASDI system was reported to have a deficit of 1.8 percent of payroll. In other words, to match promised benefits the system needed a tax rate 1.8 percent of payroll higher on average over 75 years than was scheduled by law.

This "average" gives the impression that raising tax rates or cutting benefits by 1.8 percent of payroll would make the system financially sound. This was the theory that guided the recent national commission. But nothing could be further from the truth.

The year-by-year surpluses and deficits in the system are not uniformly spread over the 75-year planning period. Neither are projected receipts roughly in line with projected outlays decade by decade. Instead, the surplus years all fall roughly between 1990 and 2010, with widening deficits thereafter. The SSA was relying on the buildup of a large trust fund between 1990 and 2010, which would be drawn down after 2010 to cover the long-term deficit until the money ran out (between 2030 and 2040). What was the system to do then, when it would suddenly face annual outlays 5 or 6 percent higher than annual receipts, with no trust fund to pay the difference?

In fact, the OASDI surpluses either would be spent by Congress or would have to be borrowed to finance HI deficits in the 1990s, and the whole OASDHI system would be bankrupt by about 2015. It would then face ongoing annual deficits of 12–15 percent of payroll under the 1982 trustees report IIB assumptions. The 1983 social security legislation did not significantly alter these prospects, particularly if the Census Bureau's new lower fertility and population estimates are employed in the calculations.

With or without HI, the 75-year average is merely camouflage for a deteriorating system. Only if the system is brought roughly into balance on a year-to-year basis can it be permanently fixed. This balancing means either slowing the growth rate of real benefits and raising hospital insurance premiums and deductibles for future retirees so that benefits only rise to 15 percent of payroll (the currently scheduled 1990 tax rate), or else roughly doubling the payroll tax to match the growth of benefits.

This fundamental imbalance in the system is largely hidden by the 75-year summary statistic. A 75-year average moves very slowly from one year to the next. Nonetheless, as each year goes by, the summary statistic decays a bit. As the planning period shifts forward, a year of near-term surplus goes by and a year of long-term deficit is added. For example, in 1985, the planning period will run from 1985 to 2060. The year 1985 will show a surplus; 2060, a deficit. In 1986, the planning period will be 1986 to 2061. The surplus year 1985 will fall out of the average, and the deficit year 2061 will be rolled in. The result is a deterioration in the system's "balance."

Every year in the trustees report, the SSA gives a list of reasons for any year-to-year change in the summary statistic. These reasons include changes in economic and fertility assumptions. One reason that appears every year is "change in valuation period." This is the admission that the 75-year average is not stable. It is a moving average that was headed toward a basic deficit of 5–6 percent of payroll for OASDI and 12–15 percent of payroll for OASDHI, under the 1982 assumptions.[4] This is why the summary statistic is a poor measure of what needs to be done for the system. This is why the tables showing the annual deficits in the system over time and the pattern that is emerging provide the only meaningful way to view the system. Bringing forward payroll-tax increases already scheduled, as was done in the 1983 social security bill, reduces the system's long-run deficit as measured by the summary statistic. But such steps do nothing to improve the system's real balance over time.

As long as the summary statistic is used as a guide to policy, we

---

[4]Under the 1983 amendments, the deficit is projected at 2–3 percent of payroll for OASDI and at 8–9 percent of payroll for OASDHI. The deficit would be larger if the calculations were based on the Census Bureau's fertility estimates.

will have periodic crises in the system. Each time the trust funds start to run out, the summary statistic will be "balanced" by some short-run transfers and tax-rate increases. Near-term benefits will be cut very little, both because it is not fair to cut benefits without adequate warning and because current retirees are active voters. This process will be enough to bring the 75-year average into "balance" with short-run surpluses and long-run deficits. Then, since the system is apparently in balance, why do anything to bring long-run benefit growth under control? And nothing is done until the next crisis, when it is again too late to touch benefits.

The President's Goals Defeated

The 1983 social security legislation was a defeat for the president's social security goals. Little was done to improve the long-run prospects of the system. Instead, Reagan was forced to accept an enlarged system, which he had eloquently opposed in the past. Coverage was extended to new federal workers and employees of nonprofit organizations, and state and local governments were prohibited from withdrawing from the system. The increase in the payroll tax rates was partly offset out of general revenues by such measures as an income tax credit. The result was a combination of higher tax rates and general revenue transfers, neither of which the president wanted.

The taxation of half of social security benefits as provided in the 1983 amendments introduced a means test into the system for the first time. Worse yet, the method of taxing the benefits was totally inconsistent with the president's desire to increase the incentives to work, save, and invest.

The correct way to tax half of social security benefits is simply to add half of the benefits to taxable income. If it is desired to give people with lower incomes special treatment and reduce their burden, part of the benefits could be excluded from tax, with only the benefits in excess of the exclusion entering taxable income. This method may push a recipient into a higher tax bracket, but the resulting disincentive would be mild compared with the way the proposal was actually implemented.

As recommended by the commission, the method of taxing half of benefits was a farce. The commission proposed that a single retiree with $20,000 ($25,000 for a married couple) in outside income from savings, private pensions, or wages be required to add half his social security benefits to his taxable income. A single retiree earning $19,999 would pay no tax on his social security benefits. A single retiree earning $20,000 would have to add perhaps $4,000 to taxable income and pay nearly $1,000 in additional tax. That is an expensive dollar of income. The marginal tax rate would have been 100,000 percent.

After loud complaints about the commission's proposal, the House version of the bill took away part of the problem and left merely a major disaster. The House phased in the taxation of half of social security benefits as other income exceeds certain thresholds. Like the commission's blunder, this action has the effect of raising the marginal tax rate on other income. But the effect is less spectacular: the marginal tax rate on income of social security recipients increased 50–77 percent. The Republican Senate could not wait to join the House in delivering this punishing blow to a major Republican constituency—retired people with a median income or higher. One Republican senator (Chafee) even got an amendment passed that included tax-exempt interest in the income measure used to determine whether the taxpayer's income exceeded the threshold! The senator was determined that no old person who had managed to save anything for his retirement would escape the net.

The result of the 1983 social security legislation was to move a retired individual with $26,000 in private retirement income from a 30 percent marginal tax rate to a 45 percent rate. A retired couple with a private retirement income of $38,000 was moved from a 28 percent to a 50 percent marginal tax rate. Social security recipients with private retirement income who are still working and have "earned income" in excess of the social security earnings limitation can face marginal tax rates in excess of 100 percent until 1990.

To understand how this happens, consider the case of the single retiree currently in the 30 percent bracket. Since his private income is above the allowable threshold, his social security income is subject to tax. For every dollar in private income above the threshold, he has to pay tax on 50 cents of social security income until he is paying tax on one-half his social security benefits.

In other words, above the threshold, every dollar of private income results in $1.50 of additional taxable income. That raises the tax rate on his additional dollar of private income by half, from 30 cents to 45 cents ($1.00 x 30% + $0.50 x 30%). The increase in the tax rate may be even higher if added income pushes him up a bracket. This continues until one-half of the benefits are taxed, at which time the effective marginal tax rate drops back down.

This approach to the taxation of social security benefits makes little sense, and it is inconsistent with President Reagan's desire to lower marginal tax rates and to increase saving and investment. Once people planning their retirement realize that the penalty for providing a private retirement income in excess of the threshold is to be hit with 50–77 percent increases in marginal tax rates, their saving rate is likely to drop. The result will be to make people more dependent on social security, thereby worsening the long-run problem.

The horror story worsens when one considers the interaction of benefit taxation with the existing limitation on earned income, which costs retirees one dollar in reduced social security benefits for every two additional dollars earned by continuing to participate in the work force. This is equivalent to an additional tax of 50 percent on additional earnings, over and above the marginal federal income tax rate. In this case, due to the loss of benefits, many retirees will experience marginal tax rates on additional earned income in excess of 90 percent. If payroll and state income taxes on additional earned income are taken into account, the marginal tax rates can exceed 110 percent. One has to ask: What happened to the Reagan administration that was going to improve incentives for people to work?

Senator Armstrong got the Senate to adopt an amendment to repeal the earnings limitation, but the Senate delayed the repeal until the 1990s. The House, however, insisted on retaining the earnings limit. The final compromise lowered the loss-of-benefit penalty for exceeding the earnings limitation from one dollar in reduced social security benefits for every two dollars earned above the limit to one dollar for every three dollars. This dropped the implicit tax on "excess earnings" from 50 percent to 33 percent, bringing the maximum tax rates faced by a retiree who continued to participate in the work force down from around 110 percent to the range of 83–98 percent.

What we have here is a form of age discrimination that perhaps manages to avoid technically violating the antidiscrimination laws, but nonetheless violates the spirit of the law. The entire thrust of the social security package is to deny the aged any incentive for being independent of the government.

The most fundamental structural factor causing social security's financial problems is its pay-as-you-go method of operation whereby all current revenues are paid out to finance current benefits, leaving only a negligible trust fund cushion. This method of operation leaves the program extremely vulnerable to adverse developments in any one of many unstable social and economic factors. Among these factors, as we have seen, are inflation, recession, mortality, and fertility.

These vulnerabilities naturally manifest themselves as social security's pay-as-you-go system reaches the mature stage. When a pay-as-you-go system starts up, a full generation of taxpayers begins to pay taxes into the system, but there are no beneficiaries entitled to benefits based on past tax payments. In a fully funded invested system, initial tax payments would be saved and invested to finance the future benefits of current workers. But in a pay-as-you-go system, since the taxes of the next generation of workers will pay for the benefits of current workers, initial tax receipts are not invested. There are consequently no significant financial demands in the start-up phase, and initial tax funds can be used to pay unexpected, unpaid for, windfall benefits to the first generation of retirees, stimulating the program's initial popularity.

As the system enters the mature stage, however, its financial background changes entirely. At this point, the program has accrued a full complement of liabilities—the enormous obligation of providing support for an entire generation of retirees—but it has accumulated no assets to aid the payment of these liabilities. Such payment of accrued benefit obligations depends solely on the maintenance of sufficient current tax revenues. At this point, it is only a matter of time before the occurrence of any one among the wide range of potentially adverse developments that can now upset the delicate balance between revenues and expenditures, tipping the whole program into bankruptcy. In this sense, eventual bankruptcy is inherently built into a true pay-as-you-go system.

In the mature stage, therefore, payroll taxes have to be constantly

69

raised to ward off threatening bankruptcy, as contrasted with the payment of unexpected windfall benefits in the start-up stage. It doesn't take great political genius to recognize that this fundamental shift will dramatically shift political attitudes toward the program. The periodic financial crises of the program in the mature stage will also sharply undermine public confidence in the system, and are thus another major factor contributing to a change in political attitudes.

Social security may cost much more than just the payroll taxes needed to finance the system. If the program has negative effects on the nation's economy, causing a loss of economic growth and national income, this loss would be an additional cost. The possibility that social security may substantially reduce economic growth and income by sharply reducing national savings has been widely studied. As we shall see, that loss of income could in fact be much larger than the cost of the program's payroll taxes.

In the following paper former undersecretary of the treasury Norman Ture analyzes social security's effect on national savings. This subject has been traditionally analyzed using what is known as the "life cycle" model. Ture finds this model inadequate and offers an alternative analysis that leads him to conclude that social security does sharply reduce national savings. By bringing to bear the standard analysis of welfare economics, Ture also finds that the program produces substantial inefficiency.

IV. Supply-Side Effects of Social Insurance

Norman B. Ture

Introduction

The social security amendments of 1983 were hailed by their authors as the ultimate solution to the financing problems of the social security system. In view of the persistence of these problems throughout much of the system's history and the frequency with which this claim has been made on behalf of legislation in the past, any skepticism one many entertain about the future financial health of the system is certainly understandable.

What is remarkable about the assertions that "this time we've really fixed the system" is that there is any occasion to make them. Why should the world's largest "insurance" system need such frequent and drastic revision of its structure of benefits and "premiums"? If the private insurance industry had produced anything like this record of financial near-disaster, it would have been clear that the market for these services had failed. Yet no matter how often it is confronted by the imminent collapse of the social security system, the American public is always assured that the system must and can be saved. What never seems to come through loud and clear is that the system is fundamentally flawed. Nor does the public at large ever seem to ask whether we really need this system and whether there are not far better alternatives.

This is not to suggest that these questions have not been raised or that they have not undergone rigorous analytical examination. Surely one of the most constructive developments of recent years is the growing conviction that the provision of most, if not all, of the kinds of benefits now afforded by the social "insurance" system

The author is chairman of the Institute for Research on the Economics of Taxation. The views presented here are the author's and do not necessarily reflect the views of IRET.

must be turned over to the private market system.[1] To a significant extent, this view has been associated with the perception that a major economic problem confronting the United States is inadequate growth in the stock of privately owned capital and that the social security system has been a major factor in discouraging saving and private investment.[2] Far less attention has been directed to whether the social insurance system is essential to remedy private "market failure" and (as a corollary) whether the private market system would more efficiently provide the same sort of insurance.

This paper deals briefly with both of these sets of questions. First, it examines the effects of the social insurance system on private saving and capital accumulation. Second, the question of whether the social insurance system affords a net gain or loss of welfare is examined. In this context, the paper also examines the benefits of a private system of retirement insurance.

What I do not attempt to cover is the difficult problem of implementing transition to a private insurance system, given the conviction that the existing system of social insurance is fundamentally flawed. It is encouraging to see the efforts that are being made by serious-minded individuals in the private sector to solve this problem. It would be even better to see the administration and Congress demonstrate real political courage by undertaking similar efforts or by at least being willing to consider the results of the existing private studies.

Social Insurance, Saving, and Capital Formation

Much of the analysis of the effects of social insurance on private saving is derived from a life-cycle hypothesis about consumption and accumulation. This hypothesis implies, among other things, that people aim at a certain income for retirement and adjust their saving out of the incomes they earn over their working lives so as to meet this income target. In this context, the social security system is perceived as exerting opposing influences on private decisions to save. On the one hand, the earnings test is thought to encourage retirement at an earlier age and to discourage part-time employment

---

[1]See Peter J. Ferrara, *Social Security: The Inherent Contradiction* (Washington: Cato Institute, 1980).

[2]See Martin S. Feldstein, "Social Security, Induced Retirement, and Aggregate Capital Accumulation," *Journal of Political Economy 82* (September/October 1974): 905–26.

after formal retirement. Given life expectancies, these responses are deemed to raise the target for retirement income, thereby increasing the desire to save. On the other hand, the social security system is perceived to provide an annuity that substitutes for the retirement income that would otherwise have to be provided by private saving, thereby reducing the incentive to save. Furthermore, because payroll taxes reduce disposable income, the life-cycle hypothesis holds that they must tend to reduce current saving. As a result, the life-cycle hypothesis implies that one cannot predict, in the abstract, whether the social security system promotes or impedes private saving. It seems to follow, therefore, that an empirical investigation is necessary to determine the true effects of social security on private saving and investment behavior.

The life-cycle model has serious shortcomings. First, it incorrectly identifies the determinants of saving behavior by considering the target for retirement income as depending on the length of one's expected retirement and on one's preretirement income. That may be a useful approach for an insurance salesman in getting potential clients to focus on their "insurance needs," but sooner or later he must inform his potential client about premiums. At that point it becomes clear that the *cost* of the benefits is a major determinant of whether, and how much, the client wants to buy. Surely the cost of acquiring any given amount of retirement income should be seen as a principal determinant of private saving. In turn, this must mean that the income targets for retirement (if they exist) must be variable rather than stationary. But if the target for retirement income is not a fixed amount, then the dollar amount of retirement benefits from social security will not necessarily have any systematic influence on the amount of private saving for retirement.

In the second place, the perception that social security retirement benefits are a substitute for the returns on private saving, however acceptable from the viewpoint of the individual, is clearly not acceptable from the aggregate viewpoint. Nothing in the social security system's intergenerational tax/pay process adds to the aggregate income-producing capacity of the economy. The total amount of benefits promised to any generation of retirees represents only a redistribution of a given amount of income; it does *not* represent any additional income produced by increments to the stock of capital. For this reason, even if a potential or actual beneficiary perceives the expected flow of social security benefits as a perfect substitute for returns on his private retirement saving, the same person and/or others must view that flow as imposing an equal drain on the rewards for working and saving. If the present value of expected benefits from social security is deemed to be an addition to the net worth of the beneficiaries, then the present value of the obligations to fund the transfers must be seen as an equal decrease in net worth. There can be no positive social security net wealth.

Those who persist in maintaining that there is a positive social security net wealth that substitutes for private-sector wealth implicitly assume that people perceive only the flow of benefits while ignoring the flow of payroll taxes that are used to fund the benefits. Such an assertion may be convenient for econometric exercises, but it certainly is not a view that accords with reality or with clear thinking.

The notion of a positive social security net wealth cannot be rescued by demonstrating that the present value of the benefits an individual will receive exceeds the present value of the payroll taxes he will have paid (including the taxes paid by his employer on his behalf). At any point in time, the total amount of benefits paid must necessarily equal the total amount of withdrawals from the income stream of some people. Only if part or all of these withdrawals are hidden from the individuals from whose income the withdrawals are made could it be assumed that the aggregate of households behaves as if there were positive social security net wealth. No Ponzi-scheme explanation can validate the notion that there is any positive social security net wealth that substitutes for private capital.

In short, the conventional approach to analyzing the effects of social security on private saving and capital formation is unsatisfactory. And the econometric exercises conducted within this framework are of little value in explaining or measuring the effect of social security on private capital.[3]

An alternative—and superior—analytical framework leads in a straightforward way to the conclusion that social security erodes private saving. One element in this analysis is the use of national income accounting to asess the *initial* impact of social security on

[3]The pattern for much of the econometric investigation of the effect of social security on saving was set by Feldstein in his 1974 paper, "Social Security, Induced Retirement, and Aggregate Capital Accumulation." The technical quality of the Feldstein study apart, the fundamental concepts employed therein are faulty, as explained above.

Gross Private Saving (GPS)—Gross National Product (GNP) less consumption and taxes. Obviously, the greater the amount of taxes, the less the amount of GPS, unless it is assumed that consumption declines in an amount equal to taxes. This would be true if and only if such taxes raised the cost of consumption relative to saving enough to induce an equal dollar decrease in consumption. A payroll tax, however, does not raise the cost of consumption relative to the cost of saving; it increases the cost of labor relative to leisure.[4] There is, therefore, no increase in the fraction of GNP that is devoted to saving as a result of the imposition of payroll taxes. Moreover, since social security benefits do not represent the value of the contribution of either current labor or capital services to total production, the immediate effect of the payroll tax in lowering GPS is not offset by an increase in GNP. Payroll taxes result in an unqualified reduction in GPS.

In the long run, the effect of social security taxes is to reduce the supply of labor, thereby reducing total output. As a result, aggregate saving, i.e., aggregate additions to the stock of capital, must also be reduced.

Social Insurance and Efficiency

In addition to the distortions discussed above, the efficiency criterion pertains to the effects of social insurance on total utility. The question then arises: does the social security system reduce an individual's utility by distorting his time paths for consumption and accumulation?

The Option of Private Retirement Insurance

To provide a conceptual framework for answering this question, consider first the results likely in a risky world with imperfect knowledge, uncertainty about the outcomes of economic decisions, and costly information, but in which there is no *compulsory* insurance system. In such a world each person must decide on his own timing of consumption and saving. These choices are based on each individual's perception of the probability distributions underlying

---

[4]It also raises the cost of labor services relative to capital services, resulting in a higher capital/labor ratio. This change in relative costs does not result from a decrease in the cost of capital services, i.e., in the amount of current consumption that must be forgone to obtain a given amount of output from the addition of another unit of capital. It does not, therefore, increase the proportion of total income that individuals want to save.

the relevant phenomena, e.g., continuity and duration of employment, illness, and other events affecting his productivity, his longevity, and the productivity of the capital he acquires. The existence of risks creates the conditions in which there is a market for a private insurance industry. Although insurance does not alter the total losses that occur, it redistributes those losses, provided the premiums equal the losses. This means that those who incur losses that are less than the mean expected value of total losses are the transferors to those individuals who have incurred losses greater than that mean.

In the individual's choice of the time paths of consumption and saving, he may include in his portfolio an insurance policy that provides him with an annuity at the time of retirement, due to either voluntary choice or illness. He may also want to include in his policy a provision for income during periods of unemployment prior to his chosen retirement date. Finally, he may want his policy to provide survivors benefits if he chooses to leave an estate.

The amount of the retirement income and income-assurance benefits an individual can provide for himself at any time will be constrained by his available resources and by the marginal productivity of his accumulated capital. Benefits do not depend on any systematic transfer of income from nonannuitants to annuitants. To be sure, some transfers are involved within the insurance system, but these transfers are random. The *average* amount of such transfers included in the benefits of all the insured must be zero. If it were other than zero for any length of time, appropriate revisions in the actuarial calculations and premiums would be made.

Opportuntities for realizing economies of scale in insurance may result in group contracts to cover some of the insurable phenomena. Group insurance should tend to reduce the transfer element included in insurance benefits, provided the groupings are based on variables relevant to the shape of the probability distribution of these phenomena. Some transfer element remains, but taking all the insured together, transfers should net out entirely. Aggregate benefits for retirement, then, are a function only of the marginal productivity of capital.

A snapshot of the private insurance system at any moment in time would reveal that retirees receiving annuities and other insurance proceeds or returns on their own assets acquired over their working lives are paying nothing into retirement funds, while workers are receiving no benefits but are contributing to such funds. This does not mean that the system is redistributing income between generations. The present generation of workers is not transferring income, in the form of retirement benefits, to an earlier, now retired, working generation. The amount of retirees' benefits depends on how much they had saved earlier and on the marginal productivity of the capital to which they have acquired claims. The present generation of workers can be said to be contributing to present retirees' annuities only in the sense that the conditions of labor supply (taken in conjunction with the stock of capital, the conditions of supply of capital, the state of the industrial arts, and the technical production relationships) determine the productivity of the capital that is the source of the benefits flow. In no literal sense are present workers financing the retirement of former workers.

The total amounts consumed and saved at any given time represent the most efficient state of affairs, given the risks and costs involved in the institutional arrangements for averting risk. Of course, some individuals will wind up with less than their optimum wealth accumulations and others with more, simply because without perfect foresight, their forecasts of the relevant phenomena are not perfectly realized. The individuals who were overanxious about the future will find that they have consumed less over their working lives than they would have, had they had perfect foresight. They will approach and reach retirement with larger accumulations than they had earlier aspired to, and if their utility functions have not changed, they might attempt a one-shot adjustment in their total assets by increasing their consumption. On the whole, however, they are likely to retire with some "excess" endowment. Other individuals, meanwhile, will have accumulated "too little," having been excessively confident during their working years. Some of these may be destitute and may be sustained either by charity or not at all.

These errors in forecasts should cancel out for all individuals. If, for some reason, there were a systematic bias in people's forecasts against the actual distributions of events around their mean values, insurance premiums would be higher or lower than required by the actual distributions. Unless individuals were completely unresponsive to changes in the cost of retirement insurance, the amount of insurance acquired would be different from the amount that would be optimum for the actual distributions. The difference in the amount of insurance proceeds actually paid, therefore, would be offset to some degree—possibly more than 100 percent—by the differences in the amount of premiums paid. Whether this offset would be perfect would depend on the price elasticity of demand for insurance, but the degree of market failure, even if the offset were not perfect, would be slight.

In admittedly oversimplified terms, the preceding discussion delineates the kind of private insurance system and how it would operate to maximize efficiency if there were no impediments imposed by the public sector. Against this outline, one can evaluate the efficiency implications of the existing social insurance system.

Efficiency Implications of Social Insurance

Suppose public policymakers insist on providing some systematic, collective remedy for the underaccumulation by those who forecast poorly. The resulting social "insurance" system might require everyone to increase his accumulation rate. The result would be an accumulation that is excessive and a time path of consumption that is too low. The social "insurance" system might be less than universal, requiring only certain groups of persons deemed to be less-than-adequate accumulators to increase their saving. In this case, the utility lost by the selected groups would not be compensated for by anyone else, since presumably everyone was already at a preferred rate of saving, given his own budget constraint and the productivity of capital. The social "insurance" system might be designed as a kind of organized charity, levying taxes on those deemed to be relatively affluent in order to transfer income to the poor. Those paying the taxes would then suffer losses in their utility. Moreover, the economy as a whole would sustain an efficiency loss in terms of changes in the composition of real output and/or in the mix of production inputs. Those receiving the transfer payments, of course, would realize utility gains.

Some gains in utility may also be realized by the taxpayers. The destitute may become less numerous, less poor, less obvious, and hence less a source of psychic distress to those who behold them; the amounts expended for private charity may be reduced; the unpleasant impact of poverty on the physical surroundings may be abated; and the inefficiently rationed demands of the poor for publicly provided services may be lessened. On the whole, however, there is no a priori case to be made that the sum of these gains would exceed the losses.[5]

[5]These alternatives should not be perceived as equivalent in terms of the efficiency losses they involve. In the first two cases, the efficiency loss results from the social

Another argument for social insurance is that the net efficiency loss from some form of compulsory retirement system disappears and is replaced by a net gain when one takes account of real-world imperfections. The argument is that it is not merely the lack of perfect foresight that prevents an individual from realizing an optimum time path of consumption and saving; more significant are the objective events over which he has no control and for which he cannot obtain sufficient information, except at extraordinary costs. That is, if he believes that information costs exceed the benefits to be derived from such information by way of better decisions about consumption and investment, and if these information costs depend on events external to his behavior, then there may conceivably be an efficiency gain in relieving him of the decision-making responsibility.

This argument obviously contains the principal elements of the externality argument for public decision making. Even so, it does not support a *compulsory* retirement system. It merely suggests that we should make available to the most poorly informed some type of retirement insurance in which premiums and benefits are based upon information that such individuals cannot economically acquire by their own efforts, and that we should advise them of the pertinent costs and benefits.

Against the criteria suggested above, the social security system emerges as seriously deficient. The system is compulsory and well-nigh universal. Participation, therefore, implies nothing about any covered individual's preferences and perceptions regarding an optimum time path of consumption and saving. While the required participation undoubtedly conforms closely with the preferences of some of the covered individuals, it defies credulity that it does so for most of them. To assume the contrary requires one to assume an extraordinarily close clustering of participants' preferences around the mean values of the principal elements of the system.

Beyond this basic violation of efficiency, the social security system involves other significant efficiency losses. Since the amount of "premiums" paid by any covered employee is a function only of the amount of his wages or salary (given the statutory rate and base provisions), there is no a priori basis for assuming that the premium

requirement for too much private saving, too much additional private capital. In the last case, by contrast, the tax/pay system must result in too little saving and too little private capital accumulation.

he pays at any time conforms with his preferred allocation between consumption and saving. Similarly, there is no basis for claiming that the path of consumption or saving implied by the premiums is congruent with is preferred path.

Moreover, one would have to assume lack of conformance even if the annuity accumulated on the employee's behalf were equivalent to what he might obtain independently in the marketplace with the same annual premium payments. Of course, his "premium" payments do not purchase a market-determined annuity for him, but rather an annuity that is based principally on his years of coverage and on his taxable earnings in covered employment. Thus, regardless of whether the social security trust funds are on an "actuarially" sound basis—in the sense that their total receipts are adequate to fund the total benefits paid—no present-day contributor is likely to receive benefits determined by a market rate of interest on his "premiums." And no present-day beneficiary's benefits are likely to be equal to the annuity that would result from the wealth accumulated, at market-determined rates, from the premiums he actually paid. In other words, for no given individual are the premiums paid and the benefits received likely to be related by the market measure of the marginal productivity of capital.

As in the case of private insurance, some covered employees will eventually wind up as transferors and some as transferees under the social "insurance" system.[6] In contrast with private insurance, however, the income transfers are not functions of the difference between an individual's actual experience and the mean value of the probability distributions of the relevant events that determine how much he actually has accumulated and how much he is contractually obligated to receive. In the case of private annuities (ignoring survivors benefits), the transferors are those who die before they reach the actuarial mean life expectancy that determined the amount of premium required per dollar of annuity, while the transferees are those who live longer than that mean. In the case of social security, on the other hand, the transferors and the transferees are distributed with respect to a much larger number of variables: how much they would have saved otherwise, into what kind of capital or claims they would have channeled their savings, when they

---

[6]The *intragenerational* transfer under social insurance is discussed in Anthony Pellechio and Gordon Goodfellow, "Individual Gains and Losses from Social Security before and after the 1983 Amendments," *Cato Journal* 3 (Fall 1983): 417–42.

would have chosen to begin to receive annuity benefits, how much survivors benefits they would have opted for, and so on, as well as their longevity.

Conclusion

Whether assessed in terms of how it impairs growth in the stock of capital and how it distorts the labor/leisure choice or in terms of the more traditional criteria of welfare economics, the social insurance system is basically deficient. These deficiencies are not addressed by concerns about the present or prospective balance in the trust funds, i.e., about the adequacy of financing the legislated benefits. The 1983 social security legislation has not repaired the fundamental flaws in the social insurance system; indeed, it has augmented them.

The same sort of examination that reveals the inefficiencies of social insurance urges that the private insurance industry, if unencumbered by a large government presence, would far more effectively satisfy demands for retirement income and income assurance. Notwithstanding the differences in analytical approach, there is a growing consensus that ultimately the government should—some would insist must—relinquish its dominance in this aspect of our economic life. At minimum, the social security system should revert to what it was originally intended to be: a supplement to private provision for retirement and income protection.

EDITOR'S COMMENT

As Ture indicates, the impact of social security on national savings is usually analyzed on the basis of the "life cycle" model. This model suggests that workers seek to even out their consumption over their lives, borrowing during the early, low-earning years of their careers, saving during the later, high-earning years, and consuming that saving in retirement. Even on the basis of this traditional analysis, social security still appears to reduce national savings sharply.

To see this, consider the perspective of an individual worker. Paying into social security seems to the worker to be the same in effect as saving for retirement: he pays into the program now and receives retirement benefits later. Consequently, he can be expected to reduce the amount he saves for retirement by roughly the same amount he pays in social security taxes. Alternatively, the worker will reason that he certainly does not need to save for the portion of retirement income that will be provided by social security. Consequently, he will reduce his retirement saving by the present discounted value of his future social security benefits. Either way, since social security is run on a pay-as-you-go basis, the program does not accumulate any savings to counterbalance the decline in private retirement savings it causes. The result is a large loss of national savings on net.

With total social security taxes and spending currently running over $200 billion per year, this loss of savings could be enormous, possibly reducing total private savings by almost 50 percent.[1] Less savings translates into less capital investment, which in turn means less economic growth and GNP. Martin Feldstein, former chairman of the Council of Economic Advisers, has estimated that a savings loss of this magnitude would reduce GNP over the long run by

---

[1]Private saving in 1984 was about $270 billion. For further discussion see Martin Feldstein, "Toward a Reform of Social Security," *Public Interest* (Summer 1975): 75–95; and Ferrara, *The Inherent Contradiction*, chap. 3.

almost 20 percent.[2] This would be an additional cost of the program about four times as large as social security payroll taxes.[3]

Economists in fact generally concede that social security may have at least this one extremely negative effect on savings. Many, however, attempt to explain it away by arguing that social security has countervailing effects that tend to increase private savings, effects supposedly strong enough to almost completely balance out any tendencies to decrease savings. These supposedly countervailing effects are discussed in detail elsewhere.[4] The bottom line, however, is that they are all quite implausible and are unlikely to have any major impact in producing offsetting savings increases.[5]

The most plausible argument against the proposition that social security sharply reduces savings is the contention that without the program, workers would choose to rely on transfers from their children for retirement income, rather than saving during their working years to accumulate retirement support. In this view, social security simply replaces a private pay-as-you-go system with a public one, with no negative effect on savings. But whatever validity such an argument may hold for times past, it is clearly inconsistent with today's culture and mores. Workers have fewer children these days, and many have none at all. The nuclear family is far less stable, with weaker links among family members. Parents are getting divorced and remarried, not uncommonly more than once. Adult children live far away from their parents and siblings. In short, workers today are just not looking to child rearing as an eventual source of retirement support; they are instead investing in pensions, IRAs, and Keoghs.

While most workers today provide for retirement apart from social security through such private savings vehicles, social security *forces* workers to provide for the bulk of their retirement through a system that creates no savings. In essence, social security is a form of *forced non-saving* for retirement. It would be truly remarkable if such an anti-savings constraint were not today substantially reducing private savings.

Many economists have conducted econometric studies to deter-

[2]Martin S. Feldstein, "Social Insurance," Harvard Institute of Economic Research Discussion Paper no. 477 (Cambridge, Mass., May 1976): 33.

[3]Payroll taxes today are approximately 5 percent of GNP. *1984 OASDI Report*.

[4]Ferrara, *The Inherent Contradiction*, chap. 3.

[5]This conclusion is discussed in detail in ibid.

mine empirically whether social security has had any effect on private savings. Feldstein has conducted several such studies and has found that social security reduced private savings by close to 40 percent or more.[6] Two SSA economists later uncovered an error in one of Feldstein's key studies, and after correcting it they found no empirical support for the view that social security substantially reduces private savings.[7] Yet Feldstein in a later study corrected the error and still found that social security reduced private savings by close to 40 percent.[8] Other economists, however, have produced econometric studies showing widely varying impacts of social security on private savings, including some studies that found little or no impact.[9]

The prevailing view among economists is that this work is incon-

[6]Martin S. Feldstein, "Social Security, Induced Retirement, and Aggregate Capital Accumulation," *Journal of Political Economy* 82 (September/October 1974); idem, "Social Security and Private Saving: International Evidence in an Extended Life Cycle Model," in *The Economics of Public Services*, ed. Martin S. Feldstein and Robert P. Inman (London: Macmillan Publishing Co., 1977), pp. 174–206; idem, "International Differences in Social Security and Saving," *Journal of Public Economics* 14 (October 1980): 225–44; idem and Anthony Pellechio, "Social Security and Household Wealth Accumulation: New Microeconometric Evidence," *Review of Economics and Statistics* 41 (August 1979): 361–68; idem, "Social Security Wealth: The Impact of Alternative Inflation Adjustments," in *Financing Social Security*, ed. Colin D. Campbell (Washington: American Enterprise Institute, 1979).

[7]Dean R. Leimer and Selig Lesnoy, "Social Security and Private Saving: New Time-Series Evidence," *Journal of Political Economy* 90 (June 1982): 606–42.

[8]Martin S. Feldstein, "Social Security, Induced Retirement, and Aggregate Capital Accumulation: A Correction and Updating" (Cambridge, Mass.: Harvard University and the National Bureau of Economic Research, 1980), mimeo.

[9]See Alicia H. Munnell, "The Impact of Social Security on Personal Savings," *National Tax Journal* 27 (December 1974): 553–67; idem, *The Effect of Social Security on Personal Saving* (Washington: Brookings Institution, 1982); Robert J. Barro, "Are Government Bonds Net Wealth?" *Journal of Political Economy* 82 (November/December 1974); idem and Glenn M. MacDonald, "Social Security and Consumer Spending in an International Cross Section," *Journal of Public Economics* 11 (June 1979): 275–89; Michael E. Darby, *The Effects of Social Security on Income and the Capital Stock* (Washington: American Enterprise Institute, 1979); Louis Esposito, "Effects of Social Security on Saving: Review of Studies Using U.S. Time Series Data," *Social Security Bulletin* 41 (May 1978): 9–17; Alan J. Auerbach and Laurence J. Kotlikoff, "An Examination of Empirical Tests of Social Security and Savings," National Bureau of Economic Research Working Paper no. 730 (Washington, August 1981); Laurence Kotlikoff, "Testing the Theory of Social Security and Life Cycle Accumulation," *American Economic Review* 69 (June 1979): 396–411; "Social Security and Private Saving: Another Look," *Social Security Bulletin* 42 (May 1979): 33–40.

clusive.[10] Indeed, given their widely varying and inconsistent results, these studies are of little or no value in evaluating the impact of social security on private savings—they may in fact teach more about econometrics than about social security. It is not clear whether econometrics is capable of isolating and analyzing the impact of social security on private savings within the complex web of real world data. This is especially so when social security's effect may have been to prevent a natural increase in savings that might otherwise have occurred as incomes rose in recent decades.

Now, practitioners of econometrics may believe that policymakers should never enact reforms until such action is supported by batteries of empirical econometric studies. But inaction can be as big a mistake as any action. The world cannot stop turning until econometricians uncover what they believe are the final empirical answers, answers that they may well not even be capable of finding. Decision makers must act on the basis of their best judgment regarding social security's effect on private savings, and the best judgment appears to this analyst to be that the program is reducing private savings to some substantial degree.

It is crucially important to recognize, however, that it is not the impact of social security per se on private saving that is the critical question for public policy decision makers. Rather, the key question involves the impact of various policy alternatives on savings, and the overall costs and benefits of those alternatives. All else being equal, shifting from a public pay-as-you-go retirement system like social security to a private fully funded system would produce an enormous increase in savings, a benefit to be weighed against whatever costs might be incurred. Whether social security has reduced savings in the past is therefore not directly relevant to whether such a change should be adopted.

An entirely different negative impact of social security on the economy results from the program's payroll tax. To the extent that the tax is borne by employers, it discourages them from hiring. To the extent that it is borne by employees, it discourages them from working. Though economic analysis and empirical studies indicate that the tax is borne entirely by employers, either way the result is less employment and, consequently, less output or GNP.[11] The

---

[10]See, for example, Henry J. Aaron, *Economic Effects of Social Security* (Washington: Brookings Institution, 1982), chap. 4.

[11]See Ferrara, *The Inherent Contradiction*, chap. 2.

payroll tax is essentially a tax on employment, and here, as elsewhere, the result of taxing something is that there is less of it. The lost GNP resulting from this effect of the program would be in addition to any lost GNP resulting from the program's negative impact on savings.[12]

The burden placed on labor from social security's payroll tax is enormous. The maximum annual payroll tax is today almost $5,600, and it is scheduled to rise to almost $8,000 by the end of the decade.[13] For at least half of all workers covered by social security, the combined payroll tax is more than they pay in federal income tax.[14] In 1984, payroll tax revenues, drawn primarily from low- and moderate-income workers, were over 80 percent greater than total federal corporate and business tax revenues.[15] In a society deeply concerned about employment opportunities, this incredible tax burden on employment is absurd. Yet, without fundamental reform, the future may well hold in store only further payroll tax increases.

[12]For further discussion of the negative economic effects of the program on the labor market, see ibid., chap. 3.

[13]The scheduled tax by the end of the decade was calculated from the *1984 OASDI Report*.

[14]Benjamin Bridges, Jr., "Family Social Security Taxes Compared with Federal Income Taxes, 1979," *Social Security Bulletin* 44, no. 12 (December 1981).

[15]Council of Economic Advisers, *1985 Economic Report of the President* (Washington: Government Printing Office, 1985).

V. The Political Foundations of Social Security

Peter J. Ferrara

In evaluating the prospects for fundamental reform of social security, it is useful to consider why we have the program in the first place. Why was it started? Is there some vital function that only it can serve? What have been the sources of its political strength? What do the political foundations of the program imply for the possibilities of fundamental reform?

The Rationale for Social Security

The first point to recognize in understanding why we have the current social security program is that it has nothing to do with carefully thought-out public policy rationales. The truth is that there is no broadly acceptable rationale for the current structure of the program. As Nobel laureate Milton Friedman has stated,

> Social security involves a large scale invasion into the personal lives of a large fraction of the nation, without, so far as I can see, any justification that is at all persuasive, not only on liberal principles, but on almost any other.[1]

Of course, one cannot justify social security simply by noting that the elderly need some means of income support. Everyone always needs some means of income support, but in our society we generally rely on the private sector to provide it. Workers could simply pay into private retirement savings plans what they are forced to pay into social security, and use such funds to provide retirement support, supplemented by continued work or support from relatives in some circumstances. A justification for social security's current structure must show why we must compel everyone to

[1]Milton Friedman, *Capitalism and Freedom* (Chicago: University of Chicago Press, 1962), p. 182.

provide for most of their retirement income through social security, rather than relying on these private-sector sources.

Perhaps the most popular notion advanced to justify social security is the claim that without the program people will not provide for retirement or other insurance contingencies. People are short-sighted, the argument goes, and will not think far enough ahead to provide adequately for retirement.

It is hard to believe that the same people who engage in the countless daily transactions necessary to create and maintain the most complex, productive, highly technological economy in the world cannot be trusted to provide for their retirement and other insurance contingencies. This is especially so considering that Americans do spend large amounts each year precisely for private insurance and retirement plans. Moreover, this argument for social security is based on the highly objectionable philosophical premise of government paternalism, which, if accepted as a proper basis of public policy, would justify totalitarian control over all details of individual life to force everyone to do what experts believe is best for them.

But most importantly, even if this argument is taken completely on its own terms, it fails to justify anything like the current social security program. At most, it justifies only a simple requirement that all individuals save some portion of their income for retirement and other contingencies, but not necessarily through social security. Individuals could instead be allowed to choose among private alternatives, just as drivers in most states are required to carry car insurance but can choose to purchase it from any of many private insurers.

Another variant of the forced-saving rationale is the idea that individuals must be forced to provide for retirement through social security not for their own good, but to prevent them from imposing costs on others by failing to save for retirement during working years and requiring support from welfare in retirement. This argument is based on the philosophically peculiar and objectionable notion that those who provide charity to some individuals have the right to restrict the liberty of third parties, who are not even recipients, to ensure that they do not become recipients. In any event, this argument is ultimately inadequate for the same reason as the other: it justifies at most only a simple requirement that individuals make some provision for retirement, but not necessarily through social security.

Another rationale sometimes offered for social security holds that the system is needed to provide benefits to the elderly poor. But this rationale justifies only a welfare program with means-tested benefits paid only to those who are actually poor, not a $200 billion-a-year program paying benefits to everyone. Moreover, this rationale would seem particularly inappropriate in view of the program's many harmful effects on the poor.[2]

Another rationale sometimes advanced is based on the argument that a private market cannot provide actuarially fair annuities. An annuity guarantees an individual a certain monthly income for the rest of his life. It is the mirror image of life insurance, insuring against continued life by guaranteeing an income however long one may live. Without social security, individuals could be expected to use the amounts they save for retirement to purchase annuities.

Allegedly, however, an adverse-selection problem would always make these annuities unfair in a private market. This is supposedly because people who expect to live longer than average would tend to purchase annuities more heavily than others. To the extent that these purchasers do tend to live longer, the rates charged for annuities would have to increase to reflect the fact that the typical annuity purchaser tends to impose greater costs than does the average person. If the average person seeks to buy an annuity, he would have to pay the higher rates due to the higher costs that most purchasers of annuities impose, but which he does not. As a result, the argument goes, the average person cannot purchase private annuities at actuarially fair rates to protect him from the same old-age contingencies as social security.

This argument is based on a mistaken notion of actuarial fairness. Actuarially fair rates are based on the characteristics of the group of purchasers, not on the precise risks posed by each individual purchaser. In any insurance system, some purchasers of insurance will impose greater-than-average risks and some will impose less. But as long as the rates are based on the average actuarial characteristics of the entire group of purchasers, a potential purchaser does not face actuarially unfair risks.

Insurance companies of all types face the same problem today, and if life or auto insurance can be offered at actuarially fair rates, so can retirement annuities. Surely, those who doubt their driving

<hr>

[2]See Peter J. Ferrara, *Social Security: The Inherent Contradiction* (Washington: Cato Institute, 1980), chap. 6.

skills, continued health, or continued life will tend to buy more auto, medical, or life insurance. Indeed, people never know if they are going to live longer than applicable life expectancy data would indicate. But they do sometimes know if they are likely to live less. Consequently, the opportunity to adverse select is present to a significant degree only in the case of life insurance, not annuities.

Moreover, without social security virtually everyone would be purchasing annuities, assuming that annuities were perceived as the best private retirement alternative to social security. The actuarial characteristics of purchasers would then be virtually the same as those of the population as a whole. The average person would consequently be charged rates closely reflecting the actual costs imposed by him—rates actuarially fair in any view. If many individuals were not purchasing annuities in the absence of social security, that would mean that they had found the other possible private routes to retirement support satisfactory. People who thought that annuity rates were actuarially unfair could then rely on these other private alternatives.

Furthermore, any realistically conceivable higher costs due to annuity adverse selection would surely be minor compared with the massive advantages of private-sector alternatives to social security for today's young workers, particularly with a large portion of the population buying annuities.[3] An adverse-selection argument is hardly even relevant when the interest return alone on private accumulated retirement savings is higher than what would be paid by social security, assuming the same amounts paid into each over the worker's career, because the worker could then just rely on such interest without purchasing an annuity and still do better than with social security.

The whole argument regarding private-sector annuity unfairness is also more than a little amusing given the obviously gross unfairness of social security's annuities. As we have noted, workers do not receive equal benefits for past taxes paid into social security; two workers who have paid exactly the same taxes into the program over their working careers can receive widely differing benefits.[4] Blacks and other minorities with substantially lower life expectancies than the rest of the population also receive much lower returns

[3]For discussion of these advantages see chapters 1 and 11 of this volume and Ferrara, *The Inherent Contradiction*.

[4]See Ferrara, *The Inherent Contradiction*, chap. 6.

through social security's inflexible annuities, with no way to avoid this injustice.[5]

Finally, even taken on its own terms the annuity argument does not justify the current social security program. It justifies at most having the government offer annuities on an actuarially fair basis. If individuals nevertheless preferred private annuities or other private alternatives, this rationale provides no justification for preventing individuals from taking advantage of such private approaches rather than government annuities.

Any rational public policy foundation for social security must be implicitly based on the notion that somehow the private market just cannot generate an adequate income for the vast majority of workers for a substantial portion of their lives—the retirement years. Conservatives in particular must recognize clearly what a truly radical departure this notion is from general confidence in and support for private markets. If such a notion is valid, then indeed with a little more uncertainty or other difficulty maybe the market will be found too unreliable to support those of any age. Our analysis indicates, however, that such a notion is not valid, and those committed to expanding the role of markets and reducing the role of government can never accept such a notion.[6] Putative conservatives who advance glib, groundless, after-the-fact rationalizations for a $200 billion-a-year program are no friends of the market or limited government.

True Political Foundations

The real reason why social security was first adopted is not based on any civics-book rationale. Rather, it stems from the natural operation of social security's pay-as-you-go system and from the special deal such a system offers the first generation that adopts it—at the expense of all future generations.

When a pay-as-you-go system is begun, we should recall, the taxes of the first working generation are not saved and invested for their own benefits but are used to pay free windfall benefits to the elderly generation at the time, which paid nothing into the program. This elderly generation consequently tends to support adoption of the program. Moreover, those near retirement have to pay social

[5]See discussion in chapter 11 of this volume and Ferrara, *The Inherent Contradiction,* chaps. 4 and 6.

[6]See Ferrara, *The Inherent Contradiction,* chaps. 4 and 9.

security taxes only for a few years before they too start receiving full benefits, and consequently they also tend to support the program's adoption. Only those younger workers who have to pay social security taxes for most of their careers tend to oppose the program. When their opposition, along with social traditions or legal barriers against government intrusion into the private economy, is insufficient, a public pay-as-you-go retirement system will tend to be adopted.

In the years after the system is adopted, those in the first retired generation and most of those in the work force at the time receive high, above-market returns because they have to pay the program's taxes for only part of their working careers. During this start-up period, moreover, the program faces no financing problems or threats of bankruptcy, with a whole working generation's tax payments flowing in and with few accrued benefit claims. On the contrary, the program appears to be running huge surpluses, and the only question is whether the government can shovel out benefits fast enough to people who were not expecting them and who, therefore, will be grateful for whatever they get. There is no pressure to increase taxes, and, indeed, implementation of the full tax burden of the program can be delayed due to the low accrued benefit demands, creating in effect a phase-in of the program. These features of the start-up phase of a pay-as-you-go system result in the widespread popularity of the program during this period.

But once the next working generation retires, after paying taxes into the system throughout all its working years, the mature phase of the pay-as-you-go system begins and the picture changes dramatically.

First, serious financing problems and threats of bankruptcy begin to appear regularly. As discussed in the *Comment* following chapter 2, in the mature phase enormous liabilities owed to current retirees have been accrued, with no funds saved to finance them. The program consequently becomes vulnerable to significant changes in any of a number of unstable economic, demographic, and other factors, and these changes can tip into deficit the precarious balance between incoming taxes and outgoing benefits. Sharp increases in unemployment or inflation; steep recessions; slower real wage growth; marked reductions in work force participation by the elderly, teenagers, women, or minorities; substantial life-extension through medical breakthroughs; lower birth rates over the long-term—all can edge a mature pay-as-you-go system into bankruptcy, even if these trends reverse themselves later. The instability of these potentially disruptive factors means that serious financing crises will inevitably occur.

Second, there is constant financial pressure for tax increases, rather than room for windfall benefit increases. With a full complement of benefits owed to current retirees, there are no longer any unclaimed surpluses or free benefits to pay out. The issue instead becomes whether taxes from current workers will be sufficient to pay liabilities owed to current retirees. The periodic financing crises in the mature stage require periodic tax increases just to maintain benefits at expected levels.

Third, the rate of return paid by the pay-as-you-go system naturally falls below market returns, and the program becomes a bad deal. As discussed in chapter 1, over time the initial high returns enjoyed by early retirees begin to fall as workers retire who paid taxes into the program for more and more of their working years. Once workers begin retiring who had to pay social security taxes for their entire careers, the program's benefits will naturally represent a low return on their tax dollars. Indeed, this return would likely be a mere fraction of market returns, possibly even negative.

Finally, the development of the above problems exacerbates other problems. As the returns paid through social security fall, inequities in the program's benefit structure become much more troubling than when everyone was receiving far more than they paid in taxes in any event. With periodic financial crises threatening the system, a naturally politicized public retirement program becomes even more of a political football. The payroll tax increases necessitated by these financial crises add to the economic damage caused by the system, further reduce workers' control over their incomes, and expand the restrictions of individual liberty involved in the program.

While these overwhelming problems will plague the second and, indeed, all future working generations after the introduction of a pay-as-you-go system, those generations cannot vote at the time the program is adopted. In large part, the second working generation would not even have been born yet. Consequently, their future problems will tend not to prevent the program from being adopted.

The true reason for the adoption of a pay-as-you-go social security system can, therefore, be stated simply: it allows the first elderly generation and much of the first working generation—a majority of voters at any particular time—to obtain free, windfall benefits at the great expense of future generations, which cannot yet vote to protect themselves. The system is in effect a way for initial generations to tax future, unrepresented generations, as the initial generations agree to accrue liabilities owed to themselves that must be paid by the taxes of future generations. For future generations this is much worse even than taxation without representation, for they are saddled with all the problems of the mature pay-as-you-go system as well.

This is hardly an attractive rationale or foundation for social security. The program can be seen as the result of an "externality" in the political realm perfectly analogous to externalities in the economic realm. The political externality arises because the first generations receive the initial benefits of the system but do not pay the full costs, while those who bear the later costs are not yet around to object. The true cost of the system is consequently not taken into account, and it is instituted and expanded even though great harm is thereby done to the nation over the long run. This externality thus produces "political failure," just as externalities in the marketplace produce so-called market failure.

This analysis also explains how the program is indeed like a Ponzi scheme or chain letter. Through such devices initial participants convince later participants to transfer funds to them in return for larger transfers from a supposedly larger number of future participants. Initial participants consequently do make large profits through the scheme, receiving large transfers while paying little or nothing into the system themselves. But when the number of individuals involved can no longer expand, participants can no longer receive more than they pay in and the system collapses as it becomes impossible to induce anyone to continue to pay into it. Later participants, as a result, lose the funds they contributed, for no one is any longer paying in to provide the funds needed to pay them off.

Similarly, the members of the first generation in a pay-as-you-go social security system benefit by convincing later workers to transfer benefits to them, even though they paid little or nothing into the system to get it started, promising benefits to those workers through payments into the system from later generations. Once the first generation receives its windfall benefits, there are no further means of continually expanding the system to pay above-market windfall benefits to second and later generations. True, with a government-mandated system like social security workers cannot individually choose to stop paying into the system completely, leaving later generations without any reimbursement of their contributions at all. But the later generations will at least be stuck with low, inadequate returns, rather than reaping the high windfall benefits of the first generation. Moreover, there is no guarantee that a later generation will not choose democratically to reduce participation in the system or to end it altogether, leaving some later generation with a loss of part or all of its contributions.

The above analysis also explains, as we have indicated, the past popularity of social security. The first generation of retirees following the adoption of a pay-as-you-go system receives free windfall benefits and high returns through the program, and the system appears to be running huge surpluses without any threat of bankruptcy. The program will naturally be quite popular during this period.

But our analysis also indicates that every pay-as-you-go system is born containing the seeds of its own political destruction. As the system enters the mature phase and regular financial crises begin to occur, public confidence in the program is seriously undermined. As routine windfall benefit increases are replaced with periodic tax increases and benefit cuts, widespread public dissatisfaction with the program naturally develops. As high, above-market returns through the program are replaced by low, below-market returns, the status quo will begin to appear unacceptable. One does not need to be a political prophet to see that these fundamental changes in the nature of social security in the mature phase will produce a sea change in the public's attitude toward the program.

The U.S. social security system is now entering its mature phase, and the problems discussed above are clearly appearing. As a result, one cannot judge the politics of social security in the future simply by looking at its popularity in the past. Quite the contrary, the new developments in the program are already changing public attitudes and producing a new willingness to consider fundamental reform. The original political foundations of the program are naturally crumbling, and the prospects for real reform are consequently looking better all the time.

GUIDEPOSTS FOR REFORM

At least two categories of experience can offer valuable lessons concerning how to design and implement fundamental social security reform involving increased reliance on the private sector. One is the experience of countries that have adopted such reform. The other is the U.S. experience in adopting social security in the 1930s. These experiences and the lessons they provide are discussed in this chapter, along with a theoretical and strategic framework for fundamental return.

The United States is supposedly at the forefront of major nations committed to economic organization through private markets rather than government control. Yet, while the U.S. political establishment has failed even to consider private alternatives to social security, other nations have already begun adopting reforms to take advantage of such alternatives. One of the foremost experts regarding such reform, economist John Goodman, describes below the experiences of Great Britain and Chile.

VI. Private Alternatives to Social Security: The Experience of Other Countries

John C. Goodman

Introduction

When the Greenspan Commission on Social Security Reform took up its historic mission, the nation faced two major social security problems, a short-run problem and a long-run problem. The short-run problem was relatively easy to define. The commission estimated that we would need an additional $150 billion to $200 billion over the next six years to pay for benefits that had already been promised. So in a general sense, the solution to the short-run deficit was dictated even before the commission began its work: somehow the government would have to raise $150 billion to $200 billion in additional taxes.

Like the short-run problem, the long-run problem of social security was also a financial one. But the long-run problem was much more severe. Under the "pessimistic" assumptions adopted by the Social Security Administration (SSA), we faced the strong possibility that 70 years from now between 40 and 50 percent of all taxable payroll would be needed to pay for the package of benefits that had been legislated into law.[1]

Now, extracting *half* of every payroll to support social security is a frightening prospect. There are two things that should make us view this projection seriously. First, the "pessimistic" assumptions used for short-run predictions in the past have tended to be much closer to reality than the "intermediate" assumptions of the SSA. Second, the "pessimistic" projection of the SSA is by no means the worst thing, from the perspective of social security, that could

---

The author is president of the National Center for Policy Analysis and associate professor of economics at the University of Dallas.

[1]See A. Haeworth Robertson, *The Coming Revolution in Social Security* (McLean, Va.: Security Press, 1981), p. 90.

happen. Who could have imagined 70 years ago that today we would have virtually eliminated polio, measles, and diphtheria— or that today at least half of all children with leukemia could be saved?

In a similar vein, what would happen if over the next 70 years a radical breakthrough occurred that drastically slowed the aging process and expanded the length of retirement, without correspondingly changing the number of years over which a person could engage in useful work? The result would probably be that in the next century, instead of having two workers for every retiree, we might have one worker supporting two retirees, or even three, four, or seven retirees. Such a development would not only be economically disastrous for the country, it would threaten the very political and social fabric of our nation.

I have always considered it ironic that the possibility of finding a cure for cancer and many other diseases—developments that would prevent death and prolong life—is cast in a negative light for the purposes of social welfare planning. Developments that most of us would consider optimistic, the SSA regards as pessimistic.

The long-run problem of social security, then, is much more than a matter of money. The real long-run problem is that we are placing future generations at great risk. It is much more than an economic problem. It is a moral problem. And it revolves around the question of whether we have the right to impose this risk on future generations—to mortgage the future of our children in this way.

The term "future generations" is abstract, but we must realize that children entering the first grade today will be alive and drawing social security 70 years from now. So when we talk about how the SSA will affect "future generations," we are talking about real people—the sons and daughters and grandchildren of everyone who is alive today.

It is important to note that the problem we face in the United States is no different from the problem facing every other developed country. The long-term problem of solvency in social security stems from an inherent flaw in any pay-as-you-go pension system. This system is characteristic of virtually every developed nation in the world, and the only way to eliminate or reduce the problem is to eliminate the pay-as-you-go feature or reduce it as much as possible.

There are governments in the world today that have taken major steps in this direction. Britain is one; Chile is another. Both of these nations have acted responsibly and rationally to assure that current retirees will continue to receive their full benefits; but at the same time they have greatly reduced the long-term liability of their social security systems. In both cases, these countries took steps in exactly the opposite direction from those recently taken by the U.S. Congress. They acted to solve their long-term problem *not* by forcing more workers into the system, but by going to great lengths to encourage workers to opt out.

Now if it were a law of social science that human societies inevitably construct social security systems that by their very nature are doomed to failure, then it would be futile for us to worry about the future. It would be a foregone conclusion, not subject to change. But such a development is not inevitable. Indeed, the examples of Britain and Chile provide evidence that policymakers can act responsibly to prevent—or at least greatly diminish—the kind of crisis we face today in the United States.

Contracting Out of Social Security in Great Britain

Britain has had a system of contracting out of social security (on and off) since 1960.[2] In many ways, the issue of contracting out has had a history similar to that of the issue of privatizing the steel industry. The Conservative Party favored it. The Labour Party opposed it. And when each party got into office, it put its own program into effect and reversed the policies of the previous government. In 1978, however, Britain launched the most comprehensive contracting-out scheme to date, with the endorsement of both the Conservative and Labour parties. As such it represented a political compromise.

Essentially, Britain has two types of social security benefit schemes. One requires mandatory participation; the other is voluntary. The first tier, the mandatory scheme, pays a benefit that is like a minimum income. All workers must pay in, and above a certain earnings level they receive the same benefits regardless of their earnings and the amount of taxes they contributed.

The second-tier pension scheme, however, is based on earnings. The more you earn, the greater your pension. Thus, the second tier

---

[2]For a more complete description of the British social security system, see John Goodman, *Social Security in the United Kingdom: Contracting Out of the System* (Washington: American Enterprise Institute, 1981). See also idem, "Lessons from Abroad," in *Rebuilding Social Security*, ed. Peter Germanis and John Palffy, Heritage Lectures 18 (Washington: Heritage Foundation, 1982), pp. 23–31.

is comparable to a private pension plan as we know it. In addition, and unlike the first-tier scheme, the second-tier pension is not mandatory. Private companies are granted the option of contracting their employees out of the second-tier benefit program and into a private pension plan. They are allowed to do so only if they provide their workers with a plan that provides benefits as good as or better than that which the workers would have received had they remained in the state system.

An example of contracting out is shown in Table 1. Taxes and benefits are illustrated for a worker who earned the average wage in April 1978, when the new system was put into effect. If pounds are converted to dollars using the exchange rate of one pound for

Table 1

THE CONSEQUENCE OF CONTRACTING OUT FOR A WORKER
EARNING THE AVERAGE WAGE IN APRIL 1978

	Full Participation	Contracting Out
Annual income	£4,160.00	£4,160.00
Payroll tax on the first £910	168.35	168.35
Payroll tax on additional income	601.25	373.75
Total payroll tax	£769.60	£542.10
Annual tax reduction for contracting out		£227.50

ANNUAL STATE PENSION FOR 1 YEAR OF EMPLOYMENT		
Basic component	£910.00	£910.00
Additional component [.0125 × (4160 − 910)]	£40.63	-0-

ANNUAL STATE PENSION FOR 20 YEARS OF EMPLOYMENT		
Basic component	£910.00	£910.00
Additional component [.25 × (4160 − 910)]	£812.50	-0-

Each year the contracted-out worker gets a tax reduction of £227.50 in return for forgoing the right to draw an annual pension from the government equal to £40.63 per year.

106

two dollars, then a worker who has contracted out of the second-tier pension scheme pays about $455 less in taxes each year. In return for this tax reduction, he forgoes an annual pension equal to $81.26. The amount of tax reduction is chosen so that on the average, workers will find it to their financial advantage to contract out of the system.

April 1983 marked the five-year anniversary of the two-tier system, and to date it has been highly successful. Since 1978, more than 45 percent of all British workers have contracted out of the second-tier pension scheme. Moreover, by allowing the option of contracting out, the British government has effectively cut its second-tier pension liability in half. Overall, I estimate that the government has reduced its entire social security liability by more than 30 percent by adopting the contracting-out system.

It is important to recognize what the British system of contracting out does and does not accomplish. In particular, it does not solve Britain's current short-term social security problem. There are a number of pensions-in-payment, and government must raise the revenue to pay for them. So in the short run, the government must have almost as much tax money today as it would have had without the contracting-out scheme. Nevertheless, over the long term, pension payments will be significantly reduced.

Several additional points about the British system should be emphasized. First of all, the choice to contract out is not an individual worker's choice. It is an option granted only to employers. Employers contract their workers out of the second-tier pension system by providing them with an adequate pension. Of course, it is expected that the employers will exercise this option only after consulting with their employees.

Second, private employers cannot contract out some workers and leave others in. That is, they cannot simply remove the workers who are most favorably affected by the new scheme while leaving all other workers in the state pension system.

Third, the same tax reduction is given to all workers regardless of age and income level. Table 2 illustrates the importance of this condition. The table shows the present value of full participation in the British social security system for workers at different age and income levels. For example, a single male worker who is 20 years old and earning the maximum taxable income of £6,240 per year has a present value in social security of −£22,423. Simply put, his stake in the system is negative. On the other hand, a 50-year-old

Table 2

NET SOCIAL SECURITY WEALTH FOR FULLY PARTICIPATING MALES BY AGE AND WAGE LEVEL

Weekly Wage (£)	Age			
	20	30	40	50
17.5	−8,219	−68	2,330	5,618
20	−9,722	−512	1,534	3,972
30	−15,738	−2,284	587	3,577
40	−19,512	−4,057	−360	3,183
50	−20,680	−5,829	−1,307	2,789
60	−21,297	−7,602	−2,254	2,395
70	−21,701	−9,374	−3,201	2,001
80	−21,969	−11,147	−4,148	1,607
90	−22,146	−12,919	−5,094	1,213
100	−22,281	−14,347	−6,041	819
110	−22,352	−14,828	−6,988	425
120	−22,423	−14,987	−7,752	12

NOTE: Figures are for a real rate of growth of income of 1.75 percent and a real interest rate of 3 percent.

worker who is fully participating in the system and who is making a minimum income of £910 per year has a present value in social security equal to about £5,618. Thus, as the table illustrates, British workers at different age and income levels are affected in different ways by the social security system.[3]

All workers contract out on the same terms, however. In 1978, workers who were fully participating in social security paid a payroll tax of 18.5 percent. Workers who had contracted out paid a payroll tax of 11.5 percent, so the tax reduction for contracting out was 7 percentage points. Elderly workers have less to gain by contracting out, for two reasons. First, they have a longer life expectancy and therefore can expect to draw more monthly benefit checks than younger workers. In addition, they have fewer taxpaying years left.

[3]Similar differences exist in the United States. See Martin Feldstein and Anthony Pellechio, "Social Security Wealth: The Impact of Alternative Inflation Adjustments," in *Financing Social Security*, ed. Colin Campbell (Washington: American Enterprise Institute, 1979), pp. 91–117; and Anthony Pellechio and Gordon Goodfellow, "Individual Gains and Losses from Social Security before and after the 1983 Amendments," *Cato Journal* 3 (Fall 1983): 417–42.

So contracting out is less appealing to an older worker than it is to a younger worker.

It turns out that the amount of tax reduction necessary to encourage a 20-year-old male worker to voluntarily contract out of the system would be only about 4 percentage points of payroll tax. On the other hand, to get a 50-year-old worker to voluntarily opt out of the system would require a difference of about 8.6 percentage points. Because the terms of contracting out treat all workers the same, and give all workers only a 7-percentage-point tax reduction, it is necessary to do contracting out on a group basis so that the companies that choose this option will have some young workers, some old workers, some male workers, and some female workers.

One way to understand the British system is to compare it with something that we have allowed to happen in the United States: the practice of allowing nonprofit corporations to opt out of the system. Baylor University Medical Center in Dallas, for example, is a huge medical complex that employs about 6,000 people. In the fall of 1982, they opted out of the social security system. The retirement plan that Baylor adopted was an "integrated plan," which means that it is integrated with the current social security system.

In essence, what the Baylor plan does is to establish for each worker a target level of retirement income, typically about 60 or 65 percent of preretirement income. The private plan pays survival and disability benefits not paid by the social security system. If the employee is entitled to Medicare benefits, then he receives them. If not, then the Baylor plan pays the fee necessary to enroll the employee in the Medicare program. Baylor University Medical Center calculated that in order to fund its private plan, it needed a total payroll tax of only 8.4 percent. Compare that with the 13.4 percent-of-payroll tax imposed by the social security system. Baylar calculated that over the next 10 years, it and its employees would save $92 million by opting out of social security.

There are two basic differences between what the Baylor Medical Center was allowed to do and what happens in Britain. First, in Britain you can opt out of only the retirement part of social security. You cannot opt out of other social insurance programs, such as National Health Insurance. This difference, however, is a minor one. The major difference is that under the U.S. system we have allowed an entity like Baylor Medical Center to retain $92 million as a result of opting out. In Britain the tax reduction given to companies that contract workers out is geared to be just enough to encourage opting out, but no more than that. So, for example, if we were applying the British example to Baylor Medical Center, we would not want to give away $92 million. Instead of allowing Baylor Medical Center to pay no payroll taxes as a result of opting out, we might set its payroll tax at about 5 percent. In this way, Baylor employees would still be paying something into the social security system, but their tax reduction would still be sufficient to encourage opting out.

I believe the Greenspan Commission should have proposed a plan similar to Great Britain's. If it had done so, it would have proposed continuing to encourage nonprofit institutions and state and local governments to opt out of the system, but it would have imposed an additional tax on them. In this way, the social security system would have received additional revenues in the short run, but would not have taken on the additional liability of having to pay more pensions to these workers in the long run.

Opting Out of Social Security in Chile

Chile adopted a system of opting out of social security in May of 1981. Unlike Britain, however, the Chilean scheme is an individual choice, not a company choice. Individuals are allowed to opt out of social security by putting at least 10 percent of their income into the Chilean equivalent of an Individual Retirement Account. The IRA is managed by private companies, such as insurance companies, banks, or other thrift institutions. As in the United States, there is competition among these institutions for the IRAs. At the same time, there are some restrictions on what kinds of investments the institutions can make with their clients' money.

The payroll-tax reduction for opting out of social security in Chile is 10 percentage points of income. If you remain in the system, you pay a payroll tax of 27 percent; if you opt out, the tax is reduced to 17 percent. So the 10 percent of income saved by "opting out" is theoretically the 10 percent transferred into an IRA. Finally, all new workers in Chile are kept out of the state-run social security system and are required to open up their own IRAs.

For Chilean workers who had been under the state system in the past and choose to opt out, the government gives them nontransferable bonds to cover their past contributions to the system. These bonds can be redeemed when the worker retires. At the retirement age, which is 65 for men and 60 for women, the worker may use the funds in one of several ways. For example, the worker can take

110

a series of programmed withdrawals over time from the account or can purchase an annuity with funds from the account. In the former instance, any money not spent by the retiree will belong to his or her estate. The only requirement is that a worker must leave enough in his account to guarantee him the minimum pension guaranteed by the government, which in 1981 was about $100 per month.

The system has been enormously successful. Between May and December of 1981, almost 50 percent of all Chilean workers had exercised the option to be out of the state-run system.

Principles of Contracting Out

If we are to adopt a system of allowing either contracting out of social security by companies or opting out of social security on an individual basis, there are two political realities that cannot be ignored. First and foremost is that current retirees must be paid the benefits they have been promised.

Benefits received by social security retirees are essentially dictated by a delicate political equilibrium. There is a natural political tension between the young and the old because we are in a pay-as-you-go system, and taxes paid in by the young are paid out in the form of benefits to the old. In order for the retirees to have greater benefits, higher taxes must be placed on young workers. Conversely, any proposal that drastically reduces promised benefits to current retirees is likely to be rejected.

The second political reality is that the choice to contract out or opt out must be voluntary. It must be perceived that workers are given a choice. If you opt out of the system, you get a tax reduction. In return for that tax reduction, you forgo certain claims against the social security system. On the other hand, if you want to stay in, you pay a higher payroll tax. Workers must be given the choice of staying in the system, but they must understand that their choice means that payroll taxes are going to be higher than they are today. These two political realities dictate the structure of contracting out of the scheme.

And finally, any new system must have two structural components: First, since benefit payments to current retirees cannot be changed, we must collect enough in taxes now to pay those obligations. In other words, the total amount of payroll taxes collected under a new system must equal what it was under the old system in the short run. Second, there must be a differential payroll tax. Those who remain in the system must pay higher payroll taxes than those who opt out. After all, it is the differential payroll tax that gives people the incentive to opt out.

It is worth noting that the differential payroll tax has to be larger in the short run than in the long run. When Britain adopted its system in 1978, it needed a payroll-tax reduction of approximately 7 percentage points to encourage companies to opt out of the system. Five years later, in April of this year, Britain was able to reduce that payroll-tax differential to 6.5 percent. In future years they will be able to reduce it even further. And, as I pointed out earlier, for each new generation of workers you need only about a 4-percentage-point reduction in the payroll tax to induce workers to choose the contracting-out alternative.

Conclusion

To my knowledge, the Greenspan Commission on Social Security Reform did not hear testimony from a single individual describing how contracting out or opting out works in other countries. In fact, this viable alternative to the present system was not even marginally considered.

Yet, contracting out or opting out of social security is clearly politically practical. The example set by Great Britain, a major industrialized Western nation and a democracy somewhat similar to ours, proves it. Even though Britain is more socialistic than the United States, it adopted radical reforms to reduce its long-run social security problems.

Furthermore, Britain's two-tier scheme faced no major opposition and was either endorsed or at least not opposed by the country's major trade unions. Their members had the most to gain by the new system, since it was these workers who (by and large) had the best private pension plans already in existence.

Contracting out or opting out of social security also makes a great deal of economic sense. Taxes paid into a pay-as-you-go social security scheme primarily finance current consumption. By contrast, contributions made to private pension plans provide additional funds for the private capital market. These additional funds allow increased private investment and stimulate economic growth. We owe it to ourselves to do what the Greenspan Commission did not do, and that is to take a closer look at this alternative.

The experience of Great Britain should be more instructive for the United States than the experience of Chile. Great Britain is a mature democracy, with many of the same cultural institutions and a similar degree of economic development as the United States. The reform in Chile was adopted under a nondemocratic, authoritarian, military government. Moreover, the social and economic chaos accompanying the political upheaval in Chile over the last 10–15 years would make it difficult for any system, whether a public social security system or the private alternatives, to function well in Chile's less developed economy.

Nevertheless, the experience of both countries indicates that droves of workers would choose private-sector alternatives over a public pay-as-you-go system. About half the workers in each country have so chosen. Over time, as the private-sector option becomes more familiar, workers could be expected to exercise it to an even greater degree.

Democratic adoption of the reform in Great Britain, with support of both major parties, is particularly interesting. British politics have long included a virulent strain of overt socialism. The trade unions in Britain are also far more powerful economically and politically than those in the United States, and far more militant. Yet these factors did not prevent overwhelming political support for the reform because the unions recognized that it offered a better deal for their workers. They also recognized that it created an opportunity to build stronger worker solidarity through an expanded role for union pension systems. This suggests that American labor should also be amenable to such reform.

Goodman emphasizes two further lessons. First, the reforms in both countries were based on maintaining currently promised social security benefits for the present generation of retirees. Goodman argues that this element was probably essential to the political success of both reforms and will probably be essential to political success elsewhere. Second, Goodman argues that a similarly essential element is allowing current workers the choice of staying in social security as is if they so desire. The strong political desirability of these two elements should be apparent, for together they serve to make the reform totally nonthreatening to anyone. At the same time, they do not require giving up anything politically feasible in the foreseeable future, though many may find such elements ideologically objectionable. These two points will be discussed further.

In the next chapter, economist Carolyn Weaver discusses the history of the enactment of social security and accompanying lessons for reform. Weaver has produced some of the most original work regarding such history, and has shown a refreshing imagination and optimism regarding the potential for fundamental social security reform. Her paper below documents the surprisingly broad and powerful resistance to adoption of social security in the first place. Only the special confluence of many factors, including the unique political power, skills, and commitment of Franklin Roosevelt, made adoption of the program over this resistance possible. Why such resistance, with the natural advantages of such a program for the first generation, noted by Weaver and discussed in the previous chapter?

The main factor creating the political reluctance to adopt social security, according to Weaver, was uncertainty that the benefits promised under a public pay-as-you-go system would ever be paid. Weaver argues that this indicates that present uncertainty over the future promised benefits of the system would make fundamental reform possible today. Weaver's analysis is convincing that such uncertainty played a major role in creating resistance to social security's adoption and would play a key role in stimulating support for such reform today.

But there seems to have been something even more basic and central helping to produce the resistance to social security's adoption that she describes. An even more important factor stimulating such resistance was probably the broadly held philosophical disposition of the times favoring private markets and limited government over big government programs. What is so interesting is that such philosophical beliefs, combined with other natural factors such as uncertainty, seem to have had the power to delay and perhaps forestall permanently the adoption of pay-as-you-go social security, except for the unique confluence of the special economic, social, and political factors of the mid-1930s, all despite the short-term benefits of such a system to those who first adopt it. This indicates

114

the powerful role a broadly based philosophical commitment to private markets can play today in stimulating support for fundamental reform. With such commitment apparently undergoing a revival across the country, the costs of fundamental reform, whatever they may be, become even more politically acceptable in return for the benefits.

These two points will be raised again later. We will also later examine more fundamental shortcomings of the conventional pay-as-you-go analysis described skeptically by Weaver.

VII. The Economics and Politics of the Emergence of Social Security: Some Implications for Reform

Carolyn L. Weaver

Introduction

Over the past 15 to 20 years, economists have offered a wide range of proposals for "radical" reform of social security, where "radical" is taken to imply either the explicit financing of the public debt implied by the system or else the partial or complete return to private supply. In one of the first of these proposals, offered by Buchanan and Campbell, government bonds would have been issued to the trust funds in the full amount of the system's unfunded liability—its "covert" debt obligation.[1] People would then have been permitted voluntary participation. Later, Buchanan developed a proposal to replace the payroll tax with a requirement for the compulsory purchase of social security bonds.[2] Individuals would then have been granted the option to purchase such bonds in the private sector, provided they carried a comparable return. More recently, Feldstein has argued for moving toward a fully funded-system while maintaining the government monopoly over the supply of social security.[3] Friedman, by contrast, endorses the

The author is associate professor of economics at Virginia Polytechnic and State University (on leave of absence) and a professional staff member of the Senate Finance Committee. This paper does not necessarily reflect the views of any member of the Senate Finance Committee.

[1]James M. Buchanan and Colin D. Campbell, "Voluntary Social Security," *Wall Street Journal*, December 20, 1966, p. 14.

[2]James M. Buchanan, "Social Insurance in a Growing Economy: A Proposal for Radical Reform," *National Tax Journal* 21 (December 1968): 386–95.

[3]Martin Feldstein, "The Social Security Fund and National Capital Accumulation," in *Funding Pensions: Issues and Implications for Financial Markets*, Conference Series no. 16 (Boston: Federal Reserve Bank of Boston, 1976). See also Michael J. Boskin, "Social Security: The Alternatives Before Us," in *The Crisis in Social Security: Problems and Prospects*, ed. Michael J. Boskin (San Francisco: Institute for Contemporary Studies, 1977), p. 175; and Daniel Orr, "Toward Necessary Reform of Social Security," *Policy Review* 2 (Fall 1977): 47–65.

complete privatization of the insurance functions of social security, a concept embraced by Ferrara and Wooten.[4]

The common theme of these reform proposals is that the compulsory, pay-as-you-go nature of social security in this country has resulted in significant efficiency losses for the citizenry—losses of both choice and wealth. Each of the proposals is an attempt to rationalize a seemingly irrational system; each is an attempt to put present and future generations in the position of benefiting from the fruits of their own savings and the economic growth that could be fostered.

At one level, it would seem, the political and economic climate has never been as fertile for proposals such as these. For the better part of a decade, the financing of social security has been in a shambles, and confidence in the long-term viability of the system is at an all-time low. If we know anything about the operation of pay-as-you-go systems and the probable course of mortality and longevity, the financing difficulties and confidence problems will only become more acute in the years ahead.[5]

At another level, particularly after the enactment of the 1983 social security amendments—perceived by some to have been the loss of a great opportunity for "real reform"—it is easy to fall prey to a certain fatalism. The politics of a pay-as-you-go system, or the inability to terminate or significantly scale back such a program once under way, seems so ineluctable.

In this chapter I will argue that the conventional wisdom about pay-as-you-go systems—which is basic to understanding the growth and evolution of social security—is inadequate for explaining the emergence and, by inference, the reform of the system. The transitional "gains" to be made from enacting a social insurance pro-

---

[4]Wilbur J. Cohen and Milton Friedman, *Social Security: Universal or Selective?* (Washington: American Enterprise Institute, 1972); Peter J. Ferrara, *Social Security: The Inherent Contradiction* (Washington: Cato Institute, 1980); and James Wooten, testimony, *Hearings before the Social Security Subcommittee*, National Commission on Social Security Reform Recommendations, Senate, 98th Cong., 1st sess., February 24, 1983, pp. 330–53.

[5]This theme is developed in Carolyn L. Weaver, *Understanding the Sources and Dimensions of Crisis in Social Security: A First Step Toward Meaningful Reform* (Washington: Fiscal Policy Council, 1981); idem, "The Long-term Outlook for Social Security—Continued Political Turmoil," paper from a symposium sponsored by the McCahan Foundation for Research in Economic Security, Bryn Mawr, Pa., 1982; and idem, *The Crisis in Social Security: Economic and Political Origins* (Durham, N.C.: Duke University Press, 1982), pp. 175–93.

gram financed on a pay-as-you-go basis, like the transitional "losses" occasioned by reform, are no more significant to real policy outcomes than are the *expectations* that those gains or losses will materialize.

In the midst of the economic and political upheaval of the Great Depression, uncertainty of payoff in the distant future under the new pay-as-you-go social insurance system, compared with the status quo, underlay the failure of social security to emerge prior to 1935. The same factor—uncertainty of the alternative—will be a significant barrier to reform, now that the status quo is social security. However, real reductions in the expected payoff to perpetuating the system are already observable, as are the increased uncertainties of payoff. These forces will increase the comparative attractiveness of reform.

I begin by presenting the conventional wisdom on pay-as-you-go systems. The economic and political origins of social security are then carefully examined, as they provide insight into the potential for radical reform in the coming years.

The Conventional Wisdom on Pay-As-You-Go Systems

A public retirement system financed on a pay-as-you-go basis is one in which there is essentially no accumulation of reserves; instead, benefits to the retired generation are financed by a compulsory tax levied on the working population.[6] The benefits that can be paid under such a system, which determine the rate of return on taxes paid, vary in a predictable way over the life of the system. For analytical purposes, it is useful to distinguish two periods: the "start-up" period (during which time workers pay into the system over only part of their work lives) and the "mature" state (during which time the working population spends its entire work life under the system).

Given any rate of taxation, and holding everything else constant, the rate of return on tax payments is extraordinarily high for gen-

---

[6]See Edgar K. Browning, "Social Insurance and Intergenerational Transfers," *Journal of Law and Economics* 16 (October 1973): 215–73; Joseph A. Pechman, Henry J. Aaron, and Michael K. Taussig, *Social Security: Perspectives for Reform* (Washington: Brookings Institution, 1968); and Paul A. Samuelson, "An Exact Consumption-Loan Model of Interest with or without the Social Contrivance of Money," *Journal of Political Economy* 65 (December 1958): 467–82. See Edgar K. Browning, "Why the Social Insurance Budget Is Too Large in a Democracy," *Economic Inquiry* 13 (September 1975): 373–88, for the seminal work on the politics of pay-as-you-go systems.

erations near retirement at the time of the adoption of the system. Furthermore, during the transition to a mature state, the rate of return remains well above that payable in the long term. All of the revenues collected by the government—a simple function of the tax rate and taxable wages in the economy—can be paid out to people as they retire, although they may have contributed to the system for only a brief period.

The older the system and (thus) the longer people will have paid taxes before receiving benefits, the lower the rate of return on tax payments. Ultimately, under a mature system, the average real rate of return payable is limited to the growth rate of the wage base as determined by labor productivity and employment in the economy. At least theoretically, this long-term sustainable rate may or may not compare favorably with the rate of return on private investments as determined by the productivity of capital in the economy.[7]

Once in place, the incentive to expand such a system is significant. The higher the tax rate imposed in this period (or the larger the group that is compulsorily covered), the higher the benefits payable and thus the rates of return for all of the currently retired, those nearing retirement, and those who will not be subject to the higher tax for their entire working lives. Unlike under a funded system, a decision to increase the tax rate represents a collective decision to alter the distribution of rates of return between generations—transferring income from the future generations to the present—rather than simply a decision to "save" more at a given return. In effect, expansions in the program postpone the maturing of the system and perpetuate the gains made possible during the transition.

The incentive to eliminate such a system, by contrast, is nonexistent. Once again, unlike a funded system in which accumulated reserves would be sufficient to pay off any accrued liability, eliminating a pay-as-you-go system, or setting the tax rate equal to zero, is equivalent to paying no further benefits to anyone, now or in the future. Everyone alive who has paid any taxes at all would receive a rate of return equal to minus 100 percent and would rationally oppose any such effort. Any reduction in the tax rate would likewise reduce returns.

[7]According to estimates made by Martin Feldstein, the long-term rate of growth of the wage base is unlikely to exceed 1–2 percent, whereas additional investment in the corporate-sector capital stock would yield a real pretax return of about 12 percent. See Feldstein, pp. 43, 46–47.

Taken literally, this simplistic presentation of the operation of a pay-as-you-go system implies the following:

- it always pays to create a pay-as-you-go system, although such a system may or may not make sense in the long term;
- it generally pays to expand a pay-as-you-go system; and
- it never pays to eliminate the system, regardless of how poor the return becomes.

So goes the conventional wisdom.

As a method of analyzing the evolution and growth of social security, this simple model has great explanatory power. As a method for analyzing the present "crisis" in social security, this model is equally useful. Much of the political tension today results from nothing so much as the inevitable deterioration in returns resulting from the maturing of the system, exacerbated by adverse economic and demographic changes. Coverage is nearly universal, the ceiling on taxable earnings now exceeds the earnings of the vast majority of the population (93 percent), and the only way to maintain or improve returns in the face of historically low real wage growth is to further increase taxes. But for nearly half the taxpaying population, social security taxes already take a bigger bite out of earnings than federal income taxes.[8] Given the significant redistributive elements of the system, rates of the return look especially low for young, higher-income people.[9]

---

[8]On the basis of 1979 data, the Social Security Administration found that 24 percent of households paying social security taxes, or 18 percent of all households, paid more to social security than to the Internal Revenue Service—and this is only if the employee tax is considered. If it is assumed that the employee pays the employer's share too, in the form of lower wages, 51 percent of taxpaying households pay more in social security than in income taxes. "Family Social Security Taxes Compared with Federal Income Taxes, 1979," *Social Security Bulletin* 44 (December 1981): 12–18. See also Joseph A. Pechman, "The Social Security System: An Overview," in Boskin; and Roger Leroy Miller, "Social Security: The Cruelest Tax," *Harper's*, June 1974, pp. 22–27.

[9]See, for instance, Michael D. Hurd and John B. Shoven, "The Distributional Impact of Social Security," National Bureau of Economic Research, Working Paper no. 1155, June 1983; and Orlo R. Nichols and Richard G. Schreitmueller, "Some Comparisons of the Value of a Worker's Social Security Taxes and Benefits," Actuarial Note no. 95, HEW Pub. no. (SSA) 78-11500, April 1978. Both of these studies were conducted prior to the 1983 legislation, which, by taxing benefits, raising the retirement age, and increasing taxes, further reduced returns for young, high-income workers.

As a model for explaining the emergence of social security in this country, however, something is evidently missing from the analysis. Under the original social security bill, retirement benefits were payable to people 65 and older who had contributed to the system for as few as four years. Administration estimates at the time projected that everyone retiring during this century could receive unearned benefits under the proposed distribution of taxes and benefits, with the aggregate amount of unearned benefits amounting to $500 million a year (in 1934 dollars).[10]

Yet social security, or more specifically, compulsory Old-Age Insurance (OAI), emerged from Congress in 1935 against a backdrop of significant and broad-based political opposition.[11] Already 6 years into the Great Depression and with nearly 20 million people on direct government relief, the program was challenged at every step of the legislative process. When the Social Security Act was finally passed, some 46 years after OAI had emerged in Europe, the United States became the last industrial country in the world to enact a national scheme to aid the elderly.

It is not as though Congress and the public were uninterested in the well-being of the elderly or unaware of social insurance as a mechanism for redistributing income. On the contrary, considerable attention was accorded the elderly and the problems of retirement-income security. Even before the Great Depression, 13 states established commissions to study the financial condition of the elderly and report on the advisability of public action.[12] Proposals

[10]See *Report of the U.S. Committee on Economic Security, Hearings before the Committee on Finance on S.1130*, Senate, 74th Cong., 1st sess, January 22–February 20, 1935, pp. 1334–36; and Edwin Witte, "Old-Age Security in the Social Security Act," in *Social Security Perspectives: Essays by Edwin Witte*, ed. Robert Lampman (Madison: University of Wisconsin Press, 1962).

[11]See Edwin Witte, *The Development of the Social Security Act* (Madison: University of Wisconsin Press, 1963); Arthur Altmeyer, *The Formative Years in Social Security* (Madison: University of Wisconsin Press, 1968); Paul Douglas, *Social Security in the United States* (New York: McGraw-Hill, 1939); and Carolyn L. Weaver, "On the Lack of a Political Market for Social Security Prior to the Great Depression: Insights from Economic Theories of Government," *Explorations in Economic History* 20 (1983): 294–308. See Weaver, *The Crisis in Social Security*, for a thorough development of the argument made here and the historical perspective provided.

[12]See New York Commission on Old-Age Security, *Old-Age Security*, Leg. Doc. no. 67 (Albany: J. B. Lyons, 1930), pp. 48–49, 312–24, 220–70. See also "Old-Age Pensions and Relief," *Bulletin of the U.S. Bureau of Labor Statistics*, no. 439 (1927): 431–36; "Old-Age Pensions and Relief," *Bulletin of the U.S. Bureau of Labor Statistics*, no. 491 (1929), 529–32; and Abraham Epstein, *Insecurity: A Challenge to America* (New York: Random House, 1938), pp. 532–50.

to make cash transfers to the elderly poor were debated by most state legislatures.

In part, this interest was a response to the marked demographic changes taking place at the turn of the century. For some 40 years (between 1880 and 1920), the elderly population grew faster than the overall population, and during the 1920s alone it grew at twice the rate of the overall population (reaching 5.4 percent of the total population in 1930). For the balance of the population, the median age rose from 22 to more than 26 in the period from 1890 to 1930, and the probability that a young worker would live to age 65 increased from 41 percent to 60 percent—the odds exceeding 50:50 for the first time at the turn of the century. The amount of time the young worker could expect to spend in retirement was thereby doubled.[13]

Equally important, there was an active core of advocates for the elderly in the early social insurance movement. Originating at the turn of the century with the founding of the American Association for Labor Legislation (AALL), the social insurance movement was led by social workers, social scientists, socialists, and other progressives who banded together in the name of "worker security." Workmen's compensation, national health insurance, unemployment compensation, and compulsory old-age insurance were all a part of their agenda. Designed to provide "low-cost insurance" to wage earners through a compulsory tax-transfer scheme, compulsory old-age insurance was a mechanism, said proponents, for substituting income security in the public sector for the uncertainty inherent in the private sector.[14]

The Failure of the Early Movement for Social Insurance

In this country the response to proposals for social insurance and other collective welfare schemes was poor.[15] Compulsory insurance

[13]Bureau of the Census, *The Statistical History of the U.S. from Colonial Times to the Present* (New York: Basic Books, 1970); Department of Commerce, *Historical Statistics of the U.S. from Colonial Times to 1970* (Washington: Government Printing Office, 1976); and Michael Darby, *The Effects of Social Security on Income and the Capital Stock,* Study no. 227 (Washington: American Enterprise Institute, 1979), pp. 23–26.

[14]See, for instance, Barbara Armstrong, *Insuring the Essentials: Minimum Wage Plus Social Insurance—A Living Wage Program* (New York: Macmillan, 1932); Isaac Rubinow, *The Quest for Security* (New York: Henry Holt, 1934); and Epstein. For an informative recent piece on the early social insurance movement, see Roy Lubove, *The Struggle for Social Security: 1900–1935* (Cambridge, Mass.: Harvard University Press, 1968).

[15]See Weaver, *The Crisis in Social Security,* pp. 39–41; and idem, "On the Lack of a Political Market."

was described by the Massachusetts Commission on Old-Age Pensions (in 1910), for example, as "unthinkable and distasteful."[16] For the Pennsylvania Chamber of Commerce (in 1924), compulsory public schemes to aid the elderly were "un-American and socialistic and unmistakably earmarked as an entering wedge of communist propaganda."[17] And for Samuel Gompers (in 1917), president of the American Federation of Labor, social insurance was "in its essence undemocratic."[18] In 1916, he vowed to assist in the "inauguration of a revolution against compulsory insurance."[19] On the eve of the Great Depression, only 1 out of the 21 reports that had been commissioned by state legislatures endorsed compulsory insurance.[20]

Predictably, the onset of the Great Depression in 1929 and the election of Franklin Roosevelt in 1932 revived interest in social insurance and, indeed, in a wide variety of proposals for using the coercive powers of the federal government to redistribute income. Advocates fueled the notion that the depression was the failure of a "wage-based" economy or, in the president's words, the product of a "disintegrating system of production and exchange."[21]

The collapse of private banking and savings institutions and sustained high rates of unemployment, particularly acute among the elderly, threatened two vital means of financial support for persons of all ages. Between 1929 and 1933, one-fifth of all commercial banks failed, and unemployment rose to 25 percent of the labor force. Between September 1929 and June 1932, the real value of all stocks listed on the New York Stock Exchange fell nearly 80 percent, and by 1934 real personal savings had fallen by $33 billion. As late as November 1934, some 19 million persons, or 15 percent

---

[16]Lubove, pp. 118–19; New York Commission, pp. 48, 312–13; and Hace Tishler, *Self-Reliance and Social Security: 1870–1917* (Port Washington, Wis.: Kennikat Press, 1971), p. 88.

[17]Cited in Lubove, p. 139.

[18]Samuel Gompers, "Not Even Compulsory Benevolence Will Do," *The American Federationist* 24 (1917): 48.

[19]Cited in Lubove, p. 168.

[20]New York Commission, pp. 312–24.

[21]Speech delivered March 5, 1934, to a meeting of the National Recovery Administration, cited in *Congressional Record*, June 22, 1935, p. 9906.

of the population, were receiving emergency or work relief from the various levels of government.[22]

Yet as the depression worsened, Congress was no more inclined to enact social security than in earlier years. The legislative response to poverty among the elderly was more direct—toward subsidization of poverty assistance programs at the state and local levels rather than the imposition of a tax on young people, many of whom were poor, in order to transfer income to the elderly, high- and low-income alike. The depression was putting great strains on the old-age assistance (means-tested less welfare) programs sprouting up across the nation. Between 1930 and 1934 alone, the yearly cost of old-age assistance rose from $2 million to $32 million, nearly 20-fold in real terms, and the number of recipients increased from about 11,000 to 235,000.[23]

By 1934, federal assistance to the elderly poor had become a major campaign issue. Organized labor and the Democratic party were joined by business organizations and the Republican party in endorsing such legislation. In that year, a bill (the Dill-Connery bill) authorizing federal aid to the states gained unanimous support in both the House Labor Committee and the Senate Finance Committee.[24] Still, no bill calling for compulsory OAI had even been introduced into Congress.

Why So Much Resistance to Social Security? Further Thoughts on Pay-As-You-Go Financing

Understanding the widespread reluctance to enact social security requires taking the conventional view of pay-as-you-go systems a step further—to account for uncertainty. Opposition to the creation

[22]Milton Friedman and Anna Schwartz, *A Monetary History of the United States: 1867–1960* (Princeton: Princeton University Press, 1963), pp. 299–419; Department of Commerce, *Survey of Current Business*, no. 8 (January 1933): 105; and idem, *Survey of Current Business: Annual Supplement, 1932*, p. 33; Bureau of the Census, *Historical Statistics*, p. 266; *Supplement to the Report of the Committee on Economic Security, Hearings before the Committee on Finance on S.1130*, p. 40; and Social Security Board, *Trends in Public Assistance: 1933–39*, p. 6.

[23]"Experience Under State Old-Age Pension Acts in 1935," *Monthly Labor Review* 34 (October 1936): 830–36; "Congress Faces the Question of Old-Age Pensions," *Congressional Digest* 14 (March 1935): 72; and *Supplement to the Report of the Committee on Economic Security*, pp. 50–51.

[24]See Epstein, pp. 533, 546; Douglas, pp. 10–11; Witte, *The Development of the Social Security Act*, pp. 5, 7; and American Association for Old-Age Security, "Both Major Parties Promise Social Legislation," *Bulletin of the AAOAS* 8 (June/July 1934): 5–6.

of the new system may well have been the rational response to the extreme uncertainty of payoff, ex ante, for most people.[25] Certainly those who were already elderly or near retirement in 1935 could plan, with a relatively high degree of confidence, on receiving net transfers from social security. Unearned benefits were typical of the start-up phase of retirement programs throughout the world, and indeed even in most private systems. And of course, with benefits likely to be payable after only minimal time under the system, the risks were low. Recognizing these factors, it should come as no surprise that when the elderly emerged as a political force in their own right in the 1930s, as epitomized by the "Townsend movement," transfers much larger than those in the social security bill were sought.[26]

For younger workers, by contrast, an intergenerational transfer scheme was only potentially profitable and the stakes were very high. The potential profitability lay in the fact that since social insurance programs were not fully funded, retirees could earn an extranormal return on their taxes for many years as income was transferred intergenerationally. Social insurance offered another potential for profit that could prevail over time. The expected returns for similarly situated workers in any particular generation were politically determined—returns did not have to be equal, since they were not constrained by market forces. Thus, depending on one's income class, or family or marital status, the return earned by particular classes of retirees could be even higher than that earned on average.

All of these benefits, however, were *contingent* upon the initially agreed-upon institutional arrangement actually coming to pass at the time of retirement—a point generally neglected in current discussions of the "gains" to be made from pay-as-you-go systems or the "losses" resulting from reform. Under an unfunded social insurance scheme, a decision at some time in the future to lower taxes

[25]This section draws on Weaver, "On the Lack of a Political Market," and idem, *The Crisis in Social Security*, pp. 49–51.

[26]The Townsend Plan would have provided payments to the elderly of $200 ($1,500 in 1982 dollars) monthly, provided they quit work and spent the entire check in the month received. The Townsend movement was said to have 3.5 million paid supporters by 1935. See Committee on Old-Age Security, *The Townsend Crusade* (Washington: Twentieth Century Fund, 1936); "Is the Townsend Plan for 'Old-Age Revolving Pensions' Sound?" *Congressional Digest* 14 (March 1935): 92–94; and Douglas, pp. 69–74.

or reduce benefits would lower rates of return not only for current retirees but also for all the workers who had already paid into the system. The same problem would result from any decline in the growth of tax revenues, such as that caused by an adverse economic or demographic change, only the effect on returns would be permanent. A simple decision—to tilt the benefit formula toward high- or low-average earners, or to cap benefits, tax benefits, lengthen eligibility requirements, or apply offsets for other pension income— could generate huge windfall losses for certain retirees. In relation to the status quo, extranormal (or even positive) returns required the assurance of political control over time and thus the ability to raise taxes to buttress returns at the time of retirement. Evidently, without legally enforceable contracts, there was no certainty of payoff, in an ex ante sense.

The experience that workers had with underfunded schemes— including public retirement systems for state and municipal employees, some company and trade-union pensions, and many of the life insurance companies that failed in the late 1800s—all clearly revealed a high degree of risk in this regard.[27] Overexpansion of benefits in the early years, when assessment rates were deceptively low, produced too high a structure of future tax rates as well as an unwillingness on the part of younger workers to continue benefit payments. Benefit reductions and outright default in such plans were commonplace. In trade-union plans, there were ongoing struggles between retirees and active workers over benefit levels as compared with assessment rates, with no clear pattern of resolution. While compulsory participation at the federal level could add permanence to an intergenerational transfer scheme by preventing voluntary exit by the young, this would be true only to the extent that younger workers lacked political control.

What did social insurance mean for organized labor? It meant a relatively certain tax on its membership (already sharply declining) in exchange for uncertain future benefits. It also meant the probable termination of its own pension plans, over which it had direct administration and control, in exchange for shared political control.

[27]"Public Sector Retirement Systems in the U.S.," *Bulletin of the U.S. Bureau of Labor Statistics,* no. 491 (1929): 542–47; "Public Service Retirement Systems: U.S., Canada, and Europe," *Bulletin of the U.S. Bureau of Labor Statistics,* no. 477 (1929): 1–170; Murray Latimer, *Trade Union Pension Systems* (New York: Industrial Relations Counselors, 1932); and Paul Studensky, *The Pension Problem and the Philosophy of Contributions* (New York: Pension Publishers, 1917).

As of 1928, some 1.6 million workers, or 41 percent of all trade unionists, belonged to unions providing old-age benefits.[28] At least during the pre-depression years, these benefit plans were perceived as both member-attracting and member-sustaining features.

Surely the Great Depression had a profound effect on the risk that people assigned to the status quo and the uncertainty associated with various social insurance alternatives. As sources of retirement income, labor earnings and private savings became considerably riskier for certain individuals—particularly those already in retirement or close to it. As a countervailing pressure, however, the shifts in political power bases occasioned by the Great Depression must have increased the uncertainty associated with the payoff under any particular social insurance proposal (with no more security than could be offered by an intergenerational "compact"). With the median age of the population just 26 (in 1930), a large proportion of the population could have made the quite rational judgment that the risk of losses under a pay-as-you-go system, when compared with the status quo, offset the potential for gains in the distant future.

The Shift in Political Power toward Social Insurance

Given this environment, there was an extraordinary shift in political power in 1934 that proved to be decisive for the enactment of social security. In that year, President Roosevelt intervened to take the political momentum behind old-age assistance to propel his own program of social security. As described by Paul Douglas, an active proponent of social insurance:

> The President wanted to delay Congressional action [on the Dill-Connery bill] in order that he might make the program his own. . . . The President's desire to combine old-age pensions with a general program of social security and his belief that a unified program should be worked out were, therefore, powerful factors in preventing Congress from passing the Dill-Connery bill.[29]

The old-age-assistance bill died in the 72d session of Congress, having failed to gain the president's support.

Shortly thereafter, on June 8, 1934, Roosevelt addressed Congress

[28]Latimer, pp. 113–16. See also William C. Greenough and Francis P. King, *Pension Plans and Public Policy* (New York: Columbia University Press), pp. 40–42.

[29]Douglas, pp. 11, 26.

on the general issue of social security. Calling for reconstruction measures to create adequate housing, jobs, and "some safeguards against the misfortunes which cannot be wholly eliminated in this man-made world of ours," the president announced his intention to formulate a comprehensive plan to "provide at once security against several of the disturbing factors in life—especially those which relate to unemployment and old-age."[30]

Three weeks later, by executive order, the president created the Committee on Economic Security (CES). Entrusted with the responsibility of fully exploring the question of social security during the remainder of the year, the CES was instructed to report to Congress with a definite program of action in January. At the top of the policy group were five cabinet members: Frances Perkins, secretary of labor; Harry Hopkins, federal emergency relief administrator; Henry Morgenthau, secretary of the treasury; Homer Cummings, attorney general; and Henry Wallace, secretary of agriculture—with Perkins named chairman. Subordinate to the committee was a technical board selected by the CES and composed exclusively of individuals from federal departments and agencies, an executive director selected by the CES, and an advisory council selected by the president. Arthur Altmeyer, assistant secretary of labor, was appointed head of the technical board; Dr. Edwin Witte, member of the economics department of the University of Wisconsin, was selected as executive director. Under the chairmanship of Dr. Frank Graham (president of the University of North Carolina), the advisory council was established to represent "the public" at large. Social reformers and other advocates of social insurance were well represented at all levels in this administrative organ of the president.[31]

The final report of the CES, transmitted to Congress on January 17, 1935, was far-reaching. Proposals for a tax-offset system of unemployment compensation and federal grants to states for mothers' pensions, care for dependent and crippled children, and public health programs were included, along with proposals for federal

[30]Text of speech in *Congressional Record*, June 8, 1934, pp. 10769–71.

[31]See Witte, *The Development of the Social Security Act*, pp. 201–2; Charles McKinley and Robert W. Frase, *Launching Social Security: A Capture-and-Record Account, 1935–1937* (Madison: University of Wisconsin Press, 1970), pp. 9–10; Douglas, pp. 27–28; Altmeyer, pp. 7–29; and Frances Perkins, *The Roosevelt I Knew* (New York: Harper and Row, 1946), pp. 278–301. For a comprehensive legislative account, see Robert Stevens, ed., *The Statutory History of the United States: Income Security* (New York: Chelsea House, 1970), pp. 59–88.

grants to the states for old-age assistance, a voluntary annuities program, and old-age insurance—the latter being the only compulsory and entirely federal program.[32] Each of the proposals was consolidated into a comprehensive bill, "the economic security bill," which was introduced into Congress two days later.

Despite the enormity of the bill before Congress (members had 2,500 pages of expert testimony and 12 volumes of technical materials used by the CES to peruse), there was no point in the ensuing legislative process during which the proposal for OAI failed to generate sharp opposition.[33] No feature of the proposal went without criticism; no fallacy went unnoticed. As Altmeyer (who would hold social security's top appointed position from 1937 to 1953) recounted, leading members of the House Ways and Means Committee approached the president "to tell him it would not be possible to get a favorable vote on this feature of the bill."[34] According to Witte, "it seemed probable" that the "OAI titles would be completely stricken from the bill."[35] On the House floor, with the Democrats outnumbering Republicans by three to one, an amendment to strike the OAI program mustered a third of the votes cast (65 to 128).[36]

On the Senate side, opposition to the administration's proposal was no less intense. On the floor of the Senate, where Democrats held a two-to-one margin, an amendment was adopted (by a vote of 51 to 35) that, if enacted into law, would have been the death knell for social security as envisioned by Roosevelt. Under the Clark amendment, employers were granted the option to contract out of the public system if they provided comparable retirement protection.[37] As one opponent said, this was the equivalent of the government "inviting and encouraging competition with its own plan which ultimately would undermine and destory it."[38] In conference,

[32]*Report of the U.S. Committee on Economic Security.*

[33]For more on this, see Witte, *The Development of the Social Security Act*; Altmeyer; and Douglas.

[34]Altmeyer, pp. 12, 34.

[35]Witte, *The Development of the Social Security Act*, p. 90.

[36]Douglas, pp. 109–10.

[37]See *Congressional Record*, June 17, 1935, p. 9442; June 18, 1935, pp. 9510–36; and June 19, 1935, pp. 9625–33. See also Witte, *The Development of the Social Security Act*, pp. 88, 102–8, 157; and Douglas, pp. 120–25, 252–65.

[38]*Congressional Record*, June 18, 1935, pp. 9532–33.

it was an unresolved issue over OAI, in particular the question of whether social security would be competitively supplied, that delayed the final passage of the entire Social Security Act. Despite all this, social security was law by summer, signed by the president on August 14, 1935.[39]

The Politics of the Legislative Agenda

Difficult indeed would be the task of finding a better example of the force of an all-or-none offer (short of the summer of 1981, when the powers of the reconciliation process were used so effectively to cut federal spending and taxes). Information was controlled by advocates, alternatives were restricted, and programs were bundled so as to preclude anything approaching a competitive political outcome. These, it is argued—not the potential "profitability" of the system—were the decisive factors in the enactment of social security in 1935.[40]

Information Control

In an atmosphere of crisis, social insurance advocates secured a measure of control over the outcome simply by dominating the information presented to Congress and the public on such issues as the "failure" of private savings and insurance institutions, the extent and causes of poverty among the elderly, and "viable" institutional alternatives. In part, this was an outgrowth of having a stronger incentive than opponents to invest in acquiring and dis seminating information on alternative social policies. The rewards to the advocate who exhibited active support for social security and helped see it through to enactment went beyond the shared benefit of having improved the world for all advocates. A job in the newly created bureaucracy, a staff position in Congress, an expanded realm for an existing agency, and jobs for students and colleagues, as well as expanded research and consulting possibilities, were but a few of the spillovers that could accrue to the advocate. Then too, advocates were frequently engaged in the types of employment (such as government agencies, social work, or universities) that

---

[39]Witte, *The Development of the Social Security Act,* pp. 159–62; *Congressional Record,* August 9, 1935, pp. 12793–94; and Altmeyer, p. 42.

[40]This section draws on Weaver, *The Crisis in Social Security,* pp. 71–76.

facilitated (or funded) research in support of government programs.[41]

Opponents had a difficult time competing. Since proposals for compulsory old-age insurance were not seriously entertained before the economic security bill, there was little incentive to invest in acquiring and disseminating counter-information and drafting alternative proposals. Likewise, there were no well-established congressional committees or subcommittees to oversee such studies. On the basis of time alone, once the CES had been appointed and its staff of experts organized, opponents simply could not compete—in the span of just five months—in turning out the volume and quality of documentary support for their proposals. At the same time, individuals had little ability to capture the benefits of costly research and lobbying. For example, since effectively blocking OAI would secure benefits for all insurance companies, or all young people, whether or not they had participated in sharing the cost, each opponent was motivated to free-ride on the activities of the other opponents.

In essence, even if the CES had not been created to supersede Congress and had not presented Congress with a complex, tied package of institutions, competing sources of information were likely to have been outweighed by the information made available by proponents of social insurance. They were the ones with the time, the funds, the expertise, as well as the ability to capture the rewards of their activities.

Agenda Control, Tie-In Sales, and All-or-Nothing Offers

President Roosevelt then bypassed Congress to establish a committee that would draft its own legislation. Staffed by an array of carefully selected cabinet members and advocate "experts," the CES had a vested interest in expanding the role of the federal government and in advancing programs with specific institutional fea-

[41]On uncertainty and information manipulation, see Gordon Tullock, *Toward a Mathematics of Politics* (Ann Arbor: University of Michigan Press, 1967), pp. 100–132; and Randall Bartlett, *Economic Foundations of Political Power* (New York: The Free Press, 1973), pp. 70–75. On the economics of lobbying, see Peter H. Aranson and Peter C. Ordeshook, "A Prolegomenon to the Theory of the Failure of Representative Democracy," in *American Re-evolution*, ed. R. D. Auster and B. Sears (Tucson: University of Arizona, 1977); and for a similar model, see Gordon Tullock, "The Paradox of Revolution," *Public Choice* 11 (Fall 1971): 89–99; and Richard Auster, "The GPITPC and Institutional Entropy," *Public Choice* 19 (Fall 1974): 77–83.

tures. The CES responded to the emerging demands for old-age security not with proposals for changes in legal, tax, or direct financial incentives for pensioning firms, for example, but by advancing a compulsory federal old-age insurance program, along with an entire array of federal/state welfare programs.

Of what significance was all of this? If the CES had simply been one of many freely competing suppliers of proposals, there would have been little significance to who drafted the bill and the particulars of the bill. But, by creating, staffing, and funding the CES with the purpose of formulating a social security program outside of Congress, elements of monopoly were created in the agenda formation process. The CES was federally subsidized to produce a bill and to produce a bill of a certain type—one that satisfied Roosevelt's expressed demands for a comprehensive, unified, and permanent program of social security, and one that was consistent with the objectives of its members.

These subsidies produced a type of power that could not be eroded by the existence of competing suppliers. Once the CES report was on the agenda, reasonable counterproposals were extremely costly to submit. In many cases, these costs would have been borne directly by participants rather than diffused through taxpayer support. And as suggested earlier, the creation of a competing proposal would have been analogous to the production of a public good for opponents. The power of the CES via subsidized information was thereby compounded by the pervasive problem of an undersupply of proposals.

More important to the nature and timing of the legislation, however, was the administration's use of standard monopoly practices, including the tie-in sale and all-or-nothing offer.[42] The tie-in sale,

---

[42]For models of agenda control in the public sector, see Charles Plott and Michael Levine, "A Model of Agenda Influence on Committee Decisions," *American Economic Review* 68 (March 1978): 146–60; Robert J. Mackay and Carolyn L. Weaver, "Commodity Bundling and Agenda Control in the Public Sector," *Quarterly Journal of Economics* 48 (November 1983): 611–36; idem, "Agenda Control by Budget Maximizers in a Multi-Bureau Setting," *Public Choice* 36 (Winter 1981): 325–52; and Thomas Romer and Howard Rosenthal, "Political Resource Allocation, Controlled Agendas and the Status Quo," *Public Choice* 33 (Winter 1978): 27–43.

On the practice of tie-in sales in the public sector, see James M. Buchanan, "The Economics of Earmarked Taxes," *Journal of Political Economy* 71 (October 1963): 457–69; and Richard Wagner and Warren Weber, "Competition, Monopoly, and the Organization of Metropolitan Areas," *Journal of Law and Economics* 22 (December 1975): 661–84.

in this context, was the exchange of the legislator's vote for a bundle of programs. The right to "purchase" one activity over which the government maintained a monopoly (such as emergency relief funds) was tied to the purchase of some other activity (namely, OAI). Rather than being able to register opposition to OAI by voting against it, the legislator had to weigh the losses associated with its enactment against the losses that would be incurred by voting down the bundle and, with it, federal relief funds. By increasing the number of politically appealing welfare programs (aid to mothers, the blind, and orphans) in the bundle, the president simply increased the likelihood of swinging opposition votes.

As an effort to restrict the scope of the legislative agenda, the ultimate check on this practice would have been a separate legislative vote on each title of the bill. Effectively utilizing the tie-in thus required the additional control over the agenda provided by the all-or-nothing offer. An all-or-nothing offer, in this context, was the implicit exchange of a legislator's vote for all items in the bundle or none at all. The legislator was thereby placed in the position of supporting the entire package as long as he assessed his position to be better than with none of the programs at all. As described by Abraham Epstein, a leading figure in the early social insurance movement, the omnibus nature of the legislation

> presented a real dilemma for earnest members of Congress. . . .
> They could not physically find the time to master the details of
> the many subjects involved in the bill. Nor could they place them-
> selves in the same category with the anti-social members of Con-
> gress in opposing the entire bill. . . . Since their choice was all-or-
> none, they voted for all and left it to the Supreme Court to separate
> the good from the bad.[43]

The power behind the all-or-none offer lay in Roosevelt's clearly stated position (or threat) that the economic security bill was to be considered as a "unified," "comprehensive" bill and that the extension of welfare to the needy aged would be unacceptable without the creation of the permanent social insurance program. This was

---

See also Gordon Tullock, *The Politics of Bureaucracy* (Washington: Public Affairs Press, 1965); William A. Niskanen, *Bureaucracy and Representative Government* (New York: Aldine-Atherton, 1971); and Ludwig von Mises, *Bureaucracy* (New Rochelle, N.Y.: Arlington House, 1969).

[43]American Association for Old-Age Security, "Social Security Bill Impractical," *Bulletin* 9 (June/July 1935): 11.

made clear at several key points, such as when leaders of the Ways and Means Committee met with the president to determine whether (given the opposition to OAI) the omnibus character of the bill had to be kept intact: "The President informed them he wanted the whole bill passed and that OAI must stay in the bill."[44] When the Clark amendment was pending in the Senate, the White House assigned expert advisers to each of several key senators in order to influence the vote, then threatened to veto the entire social security bill in the event the amendment was adopted.[45] Witte assessed the situation:

> I doubt whether any part of the social security program other than the old-age assistance title would have been enacted into law but for the fact that the President throughout insisted that the entire program must be kept together. Had the measure been represented in separate bills, it is quite possible that the old-age assistance title might have become law much earlier. I doubt whether anything else would have gone through at all.[46]

In sum, the decisive factors for the emergence (the timing and the nature) of social security were: (1) an administration committed to the program and willing and able to use the powers of the office to see it enacted; (2) a network of advocates throughout the government and at the highest levels (such as Hopkins and Perkins), well schooled in social insurance and capable of doing the necessary "spadework"; (3) the presence of a popular and time-sensitive political commodity—relief funds for states and localities—the "sale" of which the administration could tie to compulsory old-age insurance; and (4) an economic crisis working to increase the uncertainty attached to the status quo—continued employment and private insurance as mechanisms for providing retirement income.

Some Implications for Reform

Admittedly, the huge wealth transfers effected by social security over the years have created two real obstacles to reform: a dependence among the elderly on the present system, and perceptions among younger workers that high rates of return are sustainable. While these conditions tend to raise the cost of reform (particularly

---

[44]Altmeyer, pp. 12, 34.
[45]Witte, *The Development of the Social Security Act*, p. 161.
[46]Ibid., pp. 78–79.

in the near term), they do not make reform impossible or even unlikely in the longer term. The "facts of the case" are what will condition long-term pressures for reform, and the relevant facts for evaluating social security as a vehicle for providing for one's retirement are that rates of return *are* falling and that the uncertainty of payoff in the distant future *is* increasing. Recent examples abound (the taxation of benefits and the increase in the retirement age, for example) whereby cuts in social security have been possible despite their apparent unprofitability for huge segments of the population.

In 1968, Buchanan suggested that given the opportunity to choose between the present system, with its "pie in the sky" features, and genuine insurance, the individual might well

> opt for a genuine insurance scheme which allows for considerably greater certainty about rates of return on what is genuine investment, both for the individual contributor and for the group of contributors collectively. He may do so even if he fully understands and accepts the argument that . . . the intergenerational tax-transfer mechanism may possibly secure for him a net advantage. The uncertainties may outweigh the differential in possible returns.[47]

In other words, uncertainties are what will make reform possible, even at a cost. Reforms that draw on now-familiar methods of supply (such as expanded use of IRAs) will be particularly attractive.

In our present situation, radical reform of the social insurance system will require a committed administration and a core of advocates. As revealed over the past three years, our governmental institutions and the people who staff them are considerably more responsive to revolutionary ideas when they expand the realm of government than when they contract it. Who is to say, however, that there will not be a confluence of forces that promote real reform? If the extreme (and costly) uncertainty about one's financial security in old age is combined with an administration that has concrete ideas for expanding the options for young people, then— despite the transitional cost of reform—we could see real changes in our social insurance system.

---

[47]Buchanan, "Social Insurance in a Growing Economy," p. 389.

In the next paper, economist David Ranson constructs an analytical framework for evaluating social security reform. Ranson emphasizes that discussions of fundamental reform should begin not with areas of disagreement, but with broad principles on which most, if not all, can agree. The implications of these consensus principles would then logically dictate at least some basic features of the reform.

Ranson's paper elaborates a useful and innovative method of beginning to think about fundamental social security reform, and his analysis of such reform is truly insightful. Particularly noteworthy is Ranson's rejection of the idea that benefit reductions are a necessary element of any fundamental reform. And most thoughtful and insightful of all are Ranson's comments regarding the "sunk costs" of the present system.

VIII. Criteria for Reforming Social Security

David Ranson

There are two views on social security reform, both of them ardently held and widespread. One is that the system is not in any fundamental difficulty and needs only piecemeal modification. The other, to which I adhere, is that social security is in very bad shape and needs fundamental change. The approach I suggest, an "axiomatic approach," does not assume anything to begin with. It consists of a search for goals, a consideration of goals, and an examination of their consequences. It can lead to surprisingly specific conclusions.

I start with the presumption that all is not well with the social security system in spite of the most recent shoring-up that resulted from the work of the Greenspan Commission. Indeed, as Peter J. Ferrara ably demonstrates in a paper published by my firm,[1] the arrival of one more recession would immediately reopen the wounds. To change the system sufficiently to immunize it from economic change will require much more fundamental reform than policymakers have yet been willing to contemplate.

Popularity and Growth of the Program

Two points need to be considered before developing an axiomatic approach to social security reform. First, social security is admittedly a very popular program. But that is the case with any Ponzi scheme (and I have always believed that analogy to be correct). Ponzi schemes are indeed popular among early participants, and it is only in later stages that people get upset. Even when it is backed

The author is general partner and senior economist at H. C. Wainwright & Co. Economics.

[1]Peter J. Ferrara, "Social Security: The Crisis Draws Closer," *The Political Economy in Perspective* (Boston: H. C. Wainwright & Co. Economics, May 9, 1983).

by government compulsion, I believe that any such pyramid will eventually collapse.

Second, why has the social security system grown so much over the decades? My theory is that it is due, in part, to sheer bureaucratic inertia. For example, the superindexing that went into the benefit formula in 1972 is conceded by everyone to have been a technical mistake. Yet it took five years to get it corrected—even in a climate where increasing concern was being expressed about the long-range solvency of the system. During that period, some 5–10 percentage points were added to total social security expenditures, and we still have that extra spending with us today. The incentives within government are such that no serious attempt was made to reverse the rise in spending.

The Need for Axioms

Debates on social security (especially those within a political body like the Greenspan Commission) sound like fights among people who are starting from predetermined positions. The participants are not sharing ideas and modifying their views as they learn more. Moreover, the parameters of discussion take full account of the inertia to which I just referred. The debate takes as a given the system as it exists now and assumes that whatever change is suggested will have to be modest.

In a situation like this, consensus (if there is agreement at all) amounts only to a compromise reached through a bargaining process. It is not a consensus in the true sense of the word. Moreover, given the way the activism, the political influence, and the media exposure of the different factions change from year to year, 10 years can go by and the bargain that was reached originally may no longer represent the new power balance at all. So the system lurches from one bargain to another, while no one addresses the deeper problems.

The patch-up job that was achieved through the commission entailed an adversary process, the results of which seemed to please no one. How much more divisive, then, is real reform going to be? It seems inconceivable to me that general agreement can be reached on any large issue as long as each constituency argues from inside its own straitjacket of political calculation, relying on coalitions of disparate views to vote down proposals it sees as dangerous to its position. If general agreement can be reached at all, it will have to be based on more than a debate among political groups. In a sense, reform may be premature now, however high the costs of delay, because the constituencies are not yet frightened enough to let go. When they do, a common analytical approach will be urgently needed.

Calculations about what is politically "feasible" have their place. In a democracy, they help to guarantee that the views of the electorate as a whole, where leadership ultimately lies, will not be overridden. But I feel there are many circumstances in which the electorate looks to politicians for a kind of specialized leadership. It is easy to lose one's way in the maze of complexity within which the debate over the system is carried on. The leadership needed from elected representatives, then, involves much more than the ability to identify a compromise between opposing factions. It requires a sense of direction based on a reasoned analysis of where and how trouble has arisen in the past.

An approach to problem solving that might make a lot more sense would start from a common basis for agreement rather than from a set of fixed positions that necessarily spell disagreement from the beginning of the negotiations. The approach I suggest could bring the electorate itself into the decision-making process. I think it is possible for us to agree on many points, especially in terms of broad principle. The broader the principles, the more universal the agreement. I will call these principles "axioms" because that term is often used in other fields in the same way that I propose to use it here.

I do not want to add to the confusion by contributing a particular blueprint for reforming social security. A set of axioms by itself does not imply one, and there are already plenty of proposals around. But if we have axioms, we can evaluate other people's blueprints and other people's piecemeal modifications if necessary. We get an objective view of whether those plans take us closer to the axioms, the ideals, or further away.

At worst, this approach can stimulate those who are uncomfortable with the axioms I suggest to come up with and defend their own. At best, it can distinguish reform proposals that address deeper problems from those that conceal them or merely patch them up. This approach can draw more people into the thought process, including many who are now deterred by the complexity of the calculations or by the heat of the debate. Working on axioms can also enable progress to be made and conclusions to be drawn in surprisingly specific ways.

Some Suggested Axioms

There are a few caveats. The axioms I suggest here are not the only ones that make sense. My purpose will have been met if others choose to add to them. Nor are the consequences listed here the only consequences. I can claim only to have begun the process. Nor are all desirable axioms necessarily compatible with one another. However, I think that the axioms I outline are compatible. They should also elicit almost universal agreement from the electorate if they are clearly explained. Finally, I recommend that we consider axioms without trying to determine the feasibility of applying them. At this stage, that would not only be distracting but would also conflict with the main objective, which is to sketch out areas of common agreement. The four axioms I propose are as follows.

Economic Efficiency

Efficiency is a technical term dear to economists; a less hallowed term to explain what I mean is *nondistortion.* In recent years, many economists have studied the troubles of the social security system. Although their political viewpoints differ, they have brought with them awareness of an issue that was often neglected earlier: a large government program can have powerful effects on business and personal economic decisions, and thereby on the health of the economy. It seems a worthwhile goal, therefore, to move toward a situation in which unnecessary distortions are eliminated, and in which all distortions are minimized.

There are many ways in which government programs can distort the economy. However, I am concerned mainly with the overall drag on economic activity that follows from imposing disincentives on firms to use labor, on workers to earn larger incomes, and on entrepreneurs to start businesses.

In a society where taxation is already severe, it is all the more undesirable to add to the disincentives that already discourage "aboveground" economic activity. A redesigned social security system ought to restore, rather than further weaken, incentives to participate in the economy. A system that is redistributive cannot be efficient in this sense. Taxing Peter to pay Paul discourages both from working and eventually undermines the system by weakening its tax base.

There are two ways to discourage production and work effort. One is to charge a fee of so many cents for every dollar that is earned by the worker or paid by the employer. It does not matter for my purpose whether the worker or the employer pays this tax. In either case it is a fee that must be paid to allow the labor market to operate. And when you tax something you do get less of it.

The other way is to enable people to live without working. In its extreme form, such a policy would give a free pension to each person regardless of how much work he did. That does not bestir people to work harder; indeed, it removes one of the most basic drives, the incentive to work in order to survive. Social security has an element of this disincentive in it, too. A person becomes fully insured after his first 10 years of employment. By the time he is old enough to plan for retirement, the length of his employment has little to do with the size of the pension he receives.

Recognition of Sunk Costs

One of our greatest political problems is the fate of the many individuals who already receive (and many of whom depend on) social security benefits. A powerful constituency opposes benefit cuts outright because it fears establishing a precedent for much larger cuts. On the other hand, it is sometimes argued that reforming the system would necessitate reducing future benefits.

This is untrue. Perhaps continuing the system as presently designed would require benefits to be cut. But the design of a new system has nothing to do with the liabilities that (rightly or wrongly) have been accrued in the past. Even though they have yet to be paid, these claims on the present system are a sunk cost. They have now taken their place in the distribution of wealth. Whether to interfere with this distribution of wealth by repudiating some of these liabilities or to finance them somehow is a political decision. Only if we insist on saddling a redesigned system with the liabilities of the past does this apparent dilemma arise.

In a way, this axiom is an application of the old proverb that two wrongs don't make a right. Sunk costs should not be allowed to influence future decisions.

Depoliticization

Anxiety about the future, particularly among recipients of benefits, can be traced in part to a feeling of being vulnerable to short-term political forces. Correspondingly, critics of the present system often attribute its overcommitments to pork-barrel politics. Congress frequently amends the Social Security Act in minor ways, and occasionally in major ones. The system ought never to be a political

143

football. Indeed, once established, a properly designed system would be immune to the pressures of politics.

Openness

A further barrier to reform is that the system is too complicated for the man in the street to come to grips with the problems he hears so much about. A well-designed system would be simple and easily understood by its participants. The complexity of the existing benefit formulas and the sensitivity of the system to future trends in inflation, fertility, and so on, have led to confusion, uncertainty, and cynicism. Younger people doubt they will ever see the benefits to which their contributions are theoretically laying claim. Rumors of large unfunded liabilities, although officially disputed, do not die away.

There is no way for the average person to find out the size of the social security pension he has earned. He also may be unaware, for example, that the unfunded liabilities now amount (perhaps conservatively) to about $30,000 for each man, woman, and child in the population. This amount of implicit debt dwarfs anything that has ever occurred. Imagine instead a system in which it was exactly known not only how much debt had been accumulated, if any, but also how much of a pension one could expect upon retirement, as well as where the means to pay that pension would come from. Such a system would be more appealing to the average citizen than our current social security system.

Financial Soundness and Other Criteria

Conspicuously missing from the above axioms is the requirement that social security be self-financing and immune from financial threat. I omit it because it is already implicit. It is hard to imagine how a system constructed to follow these axioms exactly could get into trouble.

The benefit formula would be simple, universally understood, easily calculable, and would provide no route for subsidizing one group at another's expense. Any number of participants could be permitted to opt out without endangering the financial status of the remaining participants. No new unfunded liabilities would accumulate. It would be very difficult, perhaps even impossible, to incur a cash deficit. And such a system would help restore prosperity because it would impose little or no disincentive to work, produce, save, or start a new business. The likelihood of a crisis would be close to zero. No one would fear losing his benefits, and no one would feel that he was being cheated. The predicament of the present system could not arise.

However restrictive they may be in some dimensions, the axioms I suggest leave open many questions on which reasonable people may differ. The size of a redesigned system in relation to the economy, the types of risk that are covered, the extent to which participation is compulsory, and the extent to which the federal government delegates its own role as insuror are all open issues. Although my own preference is for a private system with maximum freedom of choice, I do not think economists have the prerogative to pronounce on such questions. If agreement could be achieved on the axioms, they should be submitted to the electorate. Finally, the axioms should be regarded as ideals to be approached, rather than achieved (although I prefer following them faithfully).

Some Consequences of the Axioms

The four axioms and some of their consequences are outlined in Table 1. First is the *efficiency* axiom. Suppose we were to design a system that did not subsidize one group at the expense of another and that did not provide disincentives to economic activity. And suppose that we pushed these requirements to the logical extreme. The result would be a program that created a one-to-one link between each dollar contributed and the actuarial benefit (in terms of discounted value) earned by that dollar. That, of course, is a very far-reaching conclusion, one that already would close off many reform proposals. However, I find it an appealing idea that would attract the electorate. The same idea appears in the IRA-type proposals that are being discussed by Ferrara and others.

The efficiency axiom has various other consequences. We would not want a social security tax as such at all, although we would still somehow have to pay off the liabilities that have accumulated. We would eliminate any means tests or retirement tests that imposed marginal tax rates on particular groups. Following this axiom would also move the social security system closer to market solutions such as privatization. The element of coercion could be reduced. But the axiom does not presume a privatized system. That question belongs to a separate axiom.

Another consequence of having efficiency as a goal is that the government would follow the same set of actuarial formulas that a private insurance system would follow if it were unregulated.

145

Table 1

AXIOMS OF REDESIGN: SOME CONSEQUENCES

Axioms	Consequences
1. *Economic efficiency* The redesigned program should be actuarially sound, and should impose a one-to-one link from future contributions to actuarial value of benefits earned.	Social security tax as such will be abolished. The retirement test will be eliminated. The system will move closer to market solutions such as privatization. Future contributions will not be tax deductible; benefits thereby earned will not be taxed. Contributions will earn interest that is tax free. Government will follow accepted private-sector formulas for assessing differences in life expectancy according to age, sex, health, and other objective criteria.
2. *Sunk cost* The program would not try to reverse past redistributions of income.	The liabilities and cash flow accrued from the old system will be acknowledged. No balance will be imposed between cash outflow and cash inflow from new contributions. Repayment to contributors of their past social security taxes will not be compelled.
3. *Depoliticization* The new system should be immune from short-term political changes.	The new benefit formula will be guaranteed by issuing bonds as future benefits are earned. The system will be isolated so as to severely limit the power of political considerations to alter the benefit formula or to cause default on the benefits.

continued

Table 1 (cont.)

Axioms	Consequences
	Market prices will be used for all valuation problems, e.g., interest rate paid on contributions, equivalence between annuities and amounts of principal.
4. *Openness* The new system should be utterly simple and understood by the electorate, and nothing should be hidden.	All noninsurance elements will be transferred to other government programs.
	Participants will be kept informed of the status of their financial stake and the condition of the system as a whole.
	Liabilities such as future pension claims will not be hidden by not being acknowledged in the unified budget.
	Arbitrary cutoff points that discriminate capriciously among similar individuals will be avoided.

Differences in life expectancy, according to an objective criterion, should be reflected in the benefit formulas; any other method is distortion.

The axiom of *sunk cost* means simply that we should acknowledge the liabilities that have accumulated up to now as a debt of the present, regardless of when they are to be paid off in the future. The accrued cash outflow should be regarded as something we have to deal with. But it is illogical to assume (as many do) that any system we build in the future must be saddled with this burden—perhaps in addition to the burden of being self-financing. One even hears the double fallacy that no future system can be self-financing because it is too expensive to pay for both burdens.[2]

The *depoliticization* axiom simply means immunizing the system from short-term political change. It means guaranteeing whatever

[2]Harry Ballantyne, chief actuary of the Social Security Administration, letter to the editor, *Wall Street Journal*, May 11, 1983, p. 35.

benefit formula is adopted by issuing bonds as the future benefits are earned. Moreover, those bonds should bear the full faith and credit of the government. They should not be repudiable. The system should also be institutionally isolated to strictly limit the political power of anyone to alter those benefit formulas or to repudiate the debt.

The fourth axiom, *openness*, requires that the system be completely understood by the electorate. Nothing should be hidden. That includes not hiding the accumulated liability, however large it may be and however much damage acknowledging it will do to the reported government deficit. The budgetary practices of the federal government do not recognize the accrual of these liabilities, but they should.

Openness also implies separating all the noninsurance elements from the present system by transferring them to some other program. It can only confuse understanding to keep the insurance and redistributive functions of the program together. Participants should be informed of where they stand in the system. In this situation one axiom assists another, because it is much easier to calculate the standing of an individual when the benefit formula consists of a one-to-one link between sacrifice and reward. A participant could receive a notice once a year, or however often we choose, stating exactly how much he has contributed, exactly how much his pension would be if he were to retire at a given age, and what the pension would be worth if he became disabled today. No one is able to make this calculation under the complex system of today.

Finally, openness implies eliminating arbitrary cutoff points that discriminate capriciously among different people and make it more difficult for each person to plan his affairs. As Paul Craig Roberts has pointed out, the 100,000 percent marginal tax rate that the Greenspan Commission thoughtlessly would have imposed on single (unmarried) social security recipients as their outside income reached $20,000 would have introduced much arbitrariness and unpredictability into their financial affairs.[3] There are many arbitrary cutoff points in today's benefit formula that are not consistent with the viewpoint that people should know exactly where they stand.

The axiomatic approach is detailed in Table 2 and in the tables that follow. Table 2 suggests some shorthand terms used in dis-

[3]See pp. 65–67 of this volume.

cussing some of the design options in later tables. Table 3 applies some of this language to outline the shape of a social security system redesigned according to the suggested axioms. Within the scope of this overall design, Tables 4, 5, and 6 lay out various options.

Table 2

TERMINOLOGY

Retirement test	A provision of the present social security system under which 50 cents of benefit is withheld for each dollar above an exempt amount a retiree younger than 72 has earned in the labor force.
Retirement insurance	A new retirement scheme that replaces the old social security tax and benefits earned thereby with a formula that ties future contributions to benefits on a one-to-one actuarial basis. This scheme may or may not be compulsory. It may be applied to all nonretired adults older than 21 regardless of work status. If the scheme is compulsory, people will be allowed to claim exemption, e.g., on grounds of disability or low life expectancy.
Retirement bonds	Nontransferable securities issued, e.g., to make explicit or to recognize the accrued claims of present workers, to recognize contributions under the new retirement insurance system, and to recognize tax-free interest earned on initial amounts with the passage of time. Guarantee status is the same as that of the recognized indebtedness of the Treasury. The government is responsible for issuing an annual statement of account to each participant.

continued

Table 2 (cont.)	
Fully insured status	The ability of an individual to prove that his total vested claims from public or private plans are sufficient, given his age at that time, for him to purchase the minimum indexed annuity when he retires.
Retirement annuity	A tax-free indexed annuity issued to a contributor upon his reaching retirement age, in an amount actuarially equivalent to his accumulated retirement bonds.

Table 3

ELEMENTS OF REDESIGN

Individuals already receiving benefits	Payments would continue, with modifications to cost-of-living adjustments (COLA).
	The retirement test would be abolished. Benefits would not be reduced if an individual chose to work after reaching retirement age.
	No future contributions to the system would be required.
Claims of individuals not yet retired	A lump-sum claim amount based on past contributions or claims earned thereby would be imputed.
	Guaranteed retirement bonds in these amounts would be issued.
New arrangements for retirement insurance	Social security tax would be replaced with a scheme of contributory retirement insurance.
	Contributions would be made non-tax-deductible.
	A minimum amount would be established for vested retirement benefits accrued in private or public sources, to confer fully insured status upon individuals.
Financial actions and future role of U.S. government	The trust fund would be abolished.
	Retirement bonds would be issued to reflect interest accrued on previous holdings.
	Bonds would be automatically converted to a nontaxable retirement annuity, commencing payment when individual reaches retirement age.

Table 4

Design Options

continued

For individuals already receiving benefits

Tax status

Benefits may be
1. tax-free,
2. subject to income tax with 50 percent exemption, or
3. subject to income tax without any exemption.

Cost-of-living adjustment

COLA may be
1. left unchanged;
2. made less generous, e.g., by switching to a consumer price index appropriate for the consumption mix of retired people; or
3. withheld until benefit cut of a predetermined percentage has been achieved.

Guarantee status

If benefits are tax-free, retirement bonds equivalent to the actuarial value of the benefit stream could be issued.

For individuals not yet retired

Computation of claim*

An individual's claim under the new system, and his starting point for accumulating additional pension rights, may equal
1. his claim under the old system;
2. the accumulated amount of his past social security taxes, plus interest;
3. his choice of (1) or (2);
4. his claim under the old system less his obligation (or zero, if the latter exceeds the former);
5. his choice of (1) or (2) less his obligation (or zero); or
6. any of the above reduced by a predetermined percentage.

Once his claim under the new system is determined, an individual will receive that amount in retirement bonds.

continued

Table 4 (cont.)

Privatization

An individual may be

1. required to leave his claim in the custody of the government until he retires, or
2. permitted to withdraw his claim if he invests enough of it in an approved private pension plan to reach fully insured status.

*According to his age and paid social security taxes, each worker has at any given time a quantifiable claim on future benefits. The amount depends partly on how the principal insurance amount is indexed to the path of average wages. It is also possible to estimate his obligation, consisting of the discounted present value of the future social security taxes he should pay through retirement age, on the basis of extrapolation of his average income.

Table 5

NEW ARRANGEMENTS FOR RETIREMENT INSURANCE

Compulsion

Contributions under the new system may be
1. compulsory for adults over the age of 21 (until they reach fully insured status);
2. compulsory, subject to exemption on grounds of disability, low life expectancy, nonresidence in the United States, and other allowable factors;
3. compulsory only for wage earners; or
4. voluntary.

Management

Contributions
1. must be paid to the federal government in exchange for retirement bonds;
2. may be paid into an approved private pension plan; or
3. must be paid into an approved private pension plan.

Recoverability

Assuming that the system is compulsory, workers
1. may not recover any of their contributions before they reach retirement age;
2. may recover any amount overcontributed (i.e., beyond what is necessary for fully insured status); or
3. may borrow back their contributions up to the accrued amount if they can prove need and make arrangements to repay.

154

Table 6
METHODS OF MEETING THE PREVIOUSLY ACCRUED LIABILITIES

1. *Borrowing.* This method would increase the deficit of the unified budget from $150 to $350 billion per annum.

2. *Temporarily increasing taxation.* This option would become much more appealing when the social security tax is replaced by a less burdensome contributory scheme of retirement insurance.

3. *Selling government assets.* The enormous holdings of unused federal land, particularly in the western states, could be sold.

4. *Reducing spending on other programs.*

5. *Repudiating other liabilities.*

NOTE: Even after scaling down the liabilities inherited under the old system, a cash outflow of $200 billion per annum will have to be met without the help of the social security tax. This liability, although it may be considerably smaller than the unfunded liability of the old system, must ultimately be paid out of the national output. General revenues will not be available to pay the debt because they are already committed. The residual liability must be financed by one of the five methods in this table.

Editor's Comment

In the next paper, economists Stuart Butler of the Heritage Foundation and Peter Germanis of the White House Office of Policy Development offer a strategic framework for achieving fundamental social security reform. Butler is one of the premier strategic thinkers among those who advocate greater reliance on free markets and private-sector institutions rather than massive, welfare-state, "Big Government," programs. One especially noteworthy element of the analysis is its rejection, as in the papers of Goodman and Ranson, of benefit reductions as a useful element of fundamental social security reform. This is becoming a broadly accepted premise of reform.

IX. Achieving A Political Strategy for Reform

Stuart Butler and Peter Germanis

Introduction

Marx believed that capitalism was doomed by its inherent contradictions and that it would inevitably collapse—to be replaced by the next stage on the ladder leading to the socialist Utopia.

Lenin also believed that capitalism was doomed by its inherent contradictions and would inevitably collapse. But just to be on the safe side, he sought to mobilize the working class, in alliance with other key elements in political society, both to hasten the collapse and to ensure that the result conformed with his interpretation of the proletarian state. Unlike many other socialists at the time, Lenin recognized that fundamental change is contingent both upon a movement's ability to create a focused political coalition and upon its success in isolating and weakening its opponents.

As we contemplate basic reform of the social security system, we would do well to draw a few lessons from the Leninist strategy. Many critics of the present system believe, as Marx and Lenin did of capitalism, that the system's days are numbered because of its contradictory objectives of attempting to provide both welfare and insurance. All that really needs to be done, they contend, is to point out these inherent flaws to the taxpayers and to show them that social security would be vastly improved if it were restructured into a predominantly private system. Convinced by the undeniable facts and logic, individuals supposedly would then rise up and demand that their representatives make the appropriate reforms.

While this may indeed happen, the public's reaction in 1982 against politicians who simply noted the deep problems of the system, and the absence of even a recognition of the underlying

Stuart Butler is director of domestic policy studies at the Heritage Foundation. Peter Germanis is senior policy analyst at the White House Office of Policy Development.

problems during the 1983 social security "reform," suggest that it will be a long time before citizen indignation will cause radical change to take place. Therefore, if we are to achieve basic changes in the system, we must first prepare the political ground so that the fiasco of 1982–83 is not repeated.

First, we must recognize that there is a firm coalition behind the present social security system and that this coalition has been very effective in winning political concessions for many years. Before social security can be reformed, we must begin to divide this coalition and cast doubt on the picture of reality it presents to the general public.

Second, we must recognize that we need more than a manifesto—even one as cogent and persuasive as that provided by Peter Ferrara.[1] What we must do is construct a coalition around the Ferrara plan, a coalition that will gain directly from its implementation. That coalition should consist of not only those who will reap benefits from the IRA-based private system Ferrara has proposed, but also the banks, insurance companies, and other institutions that will gain from providing such plans to the public.

As we construct and consolidate this coalition, we must press for modest changes in the laws and regulations designed to make private pension options more attractive, and we must expose the fundamental flaws and contradictions in the existing system. In so doing, we will strengthen the coalition for privatizing social security and we will weaken the coalition for retaining or expanding the current system. By approaching the problem in this way, we may be ready for the next crisis in social security—ready with a strong coalition for change, a weakened coalition supporting the current system, and a general public familiar with the private-sector option.

Framework for Reform

Peter Ferrara's "family security plan" provides a sound framework for reform.[2] The Ferrara plan resolves the contradiction within the existing system and provides a realistic phase-in process for a private pension plan. Recent efforts to publicize and implement the Ferrara plan, however, only confirm the fact that a successful reform

[1]See Peter J. Ferrara, *Social Security: The Inherent Contradiction* (Washington: Cato Institute, 1980); and idem, *Social Security Reform: The Family [Security] Plan* (Washington: Heritage Foundation, 1982).

[2]Ferrara, *The Family [Security] Plan*, pp. 49–73.

strategy must be designed within a framework of well-understood constraints and opportunities; otherwise we will fall into the same political traps that have discouraged many a would-be reformer.

In an effort to identify a broad framework for social security reform, the Heritage Foundation brought together various experts at a 1982 conference to discuss essential ingredients of reform. The principles and observations that emerged from that gathering can now be summarized.[3]

Calming Existing Beneficiaries

The sine qua non of any successful social security reform strategy must be an assurance to those already retired or nearing retirement that their benefits will be paid in full. It was irresponsible in the first place for the federal government to promise unrealistic benefits. But it would be even more irresponsible now to break faith with the millions of people who have based their retirement plans on these expected benefits. Instead of spreading widespread panic among our elderly, which would only undermine our efforts to reform the system, we should acknowledge the system's liabilities as a total writeoff.

From a purely political standpoint, it should be remembered that the elderly represent a very powerful and vocal interest group. This power was reflected in the 1983 bailout plan, which made no effort to address the system's underlying structural problems. One congressman, with disarming frankness, implicitly evidenced that considerable power when he explained his position on social security reform: "I have no intention of trying to explain what needs to be done, just give me a vote on something that can save the damn thing until I retire."[4]

The political power of the elderly will only increase in the future. The proportion of the population over 65 will rise steadily, from 11.3 percent today to 18.3 percent by 2030. So any proposal aimed at cutting benefits will face increasingly stiff opposition from the elderly, undermining the prospects for genuine reform. Any plan to change the system must therefore be neutral or (better still) clearly advantageous to senior citizens. By accepting this principle, we

[3]For an edited transcript of that conference, see Peter Germanis and John Palffy, eds., *Rebuilding Social Security*, Heritage Lectures no. 18 (Washington: Heritage Foundation, 1982).

[4]Rep. Marvin Leath (D-Tex.), quoting one of his colleagues in "Social Security Expendiency," *Washington Times*, March 23, 1983.

161

may succeed in neutralizing the most powerful element of the coalition that opposes structural reform.

Educating the Public

A second prerequisite for reform is to improve the public's understanding of the current program. During the 1982–83 financing crisis, there was only a vague awareness among the general population that the system was in serious trouble; the true nature of the problem and the proposed reforms were understood by very few Americans.

A comprehensive program of economic education must confront people with the facts about social security and the problems it faces. The many myths surrounding the system must be dispelled, especially the popular belief that social security is an "insurance" program financed by "contributions" that provide an "earned annuity." That many have come to rely on social security as their major or sole means of support, not realizing that it was originally intended only to supplement other sources of retirement income, is apparent from a reading of the popular press. Over the years, the program has become surrounded by a cloak of demagoguery and misinformation, woven by political leaders and interest groups seeking to further their own ends. If the public is ever to support real social security reform, this cloak must be removed.

Recognizing Successful Alternatives

Despite the unwillingness of Congress to undertake or even consider real reform, the public has shown a great deal of interest in private alternatives to social security. In a poll conducted by the Sindlinger Company for the Heritage Foundation, for instance, a majority of people surveyed said that they would favor a voluntary system. Even more people expressed the view that the private sector would be a more efficient vehicle than social security for providing pension benefits. The recent upsurge in savings put into Individual Retirement Accounts (IRAs) is further testimony to the public's enthusiasm for private pension plans. A New York Times/CBS News poll suggested that Americans had invested about $30 billion in tax-free IRAs for the 1982 tax year, which is much higher than the Treasury Department had estimated. According to the poll, nearly one out of every five employed adults had opened an account by early April.[5] Extending this option as an alternative to social

[5]Robert A. Bennett, "I.R.A.s a Hit With Taxpayer," *New York Times,* April 15, 1983, p. D1.

security could both increase savings and provide funds for long-term capital investments.

A restricted private option is now being tried in Great Britain. Britain has a two-tier retirement benefit system made up of a mandatory basic pension plan and an earnings-related pension. It is possible, however, to opt out of the earnings-related pension (but not the basic pension). The employer has the legal responsibility of making the decision to allow the employees to contract out of the plan. If an employer does decide on the contracting-out option, he is required to provide private pension benefits at least equal to those in the government program. This contracting-out scheme for the second tier has enjoyed a great deal of success. Since 1978, when it was fully initiated, nearly 45 percent of all British workers have enrolled in private pension programs.

The British system indicates that many employees are willing to choose a private retirement option in preference to a government-guaranteed plan. It also indicates that workers are willing to pay a price to leave social security. British workers who opt out of the earnings-related element of social security do not obtain a reduction in payroll taxes that is equal to the benefits they forgo. In other words, those who opt out still pay some tax to support existing and future beneficiaries of the government system.

According to John Goodman, the payroll-tax reduction available to those who contract out is carefully designed to be just large enough to encourage enough workers to opt out (thereby reducing future liabilities), while ensuring that these workers still provide considerable tax revenue to subsidize existing beneficiaries.[6] It does seem that the price people are willing to pay to leave social security is substantial. Perhaps in the United States it is large enough that those wishing to leave the system can still be required to cover a large part of the current obligations to beneficiaries without destroying the broad attractiveness of any chance to opt out, thus leading to a reduction in the system's future obligations.

A Plan of Action

The background issues discussed above suggest a political strategy to achieve basic reform of the social security system in the

[6]See above pp. 105–10, and "Lessons from Abroad," in Germanis and Palffy, pp. 23–31.

fashion suggested by Peter Ferrara. There are two main elements to this strategy.

The first element consists of a campaign to achieve small legislative changes that would embellish the present IRA system, making it in practice a small-scale private social security system that can supplement the federal system. As part of this campaign, the natural constitutency for an enlarged IRA system must be identified and welded into a coalition for political change. If these objectives are achieved, we will meet the next financial crisis in social security with a private alternative ready in the wings—an alternative with which the public is familiar and comfortable, and one that has the backing of a powerful political force.

The second main element in our reform strategy involves what one might crudely call guerrilla warfare against both the current social security system and the coalition that supports it. An economic education campaign, assisted by modest changes in the law, must be undertaken to demonstrate the weaknesses of the existing system and to allow it to be compared accurately (and therefore unfavorably) with the private alternative. In addition, methods of neutralizing, buying out, or winning over key segments of the social security coalition must be explored and formulated into legislative initiatives. The objective of this element of the strategy complements the first. The aim is to weaken political support for the present system when the next financial crisis appears. This two-pronged strategy will now be considered in more detail.

Creating a Private Model

Expanding IRAs

IRAs are a powerful vehicle for introducing a private social security system. They are extremely popular with the public. No politician wishing to be reelected would even suggest that the tax deduction for IRAs should be eliminated. Building on this strong political support, proponents of a private social security system should press for an extension of the deduction. No doubt Congress would find it difficult to reject proposals designed to allow workers to provide a more secure retirement for themselves.

The aim should be to secure legislation that not only indexes the basic IRA deduction and makes it available to all (including non-working spouses), but also allows people to take a much larger IRA deduction if it is used to purchase old-age health insurance, disability insurance, or other benefits now available through social security. Ideally, this "super IRA" would be close to the social security system in both size and structure. As the payroll tax rate increases, the maximum tax-deductible contribution to an IRA should increase to the same cash level. Similarly, the prescribed allocation of an IRA among retirement income, health insurance, and other uses should reflect the equivalent allocation of the social security tax.

The reason for designing a super-IRA law with these restrictions is purely political. Expanding the IRA system in this way would make it a private prototype of social security. People could then compare the two alternatives. The public would gradually become more familiar with the private option, and would no doubt view it as a parallel system. If that did happen, it would be far easier than it is now to persuade people to adopt the private plan as their principal source of old-age insurance and retirement income.

Coalition Building

Building a constituency for social security reform requires mobilizing the various coalitions that stand to benefit from the change. Such a constituency is already extensive, but mobilizing it could become a self-generating process. If an extension in the IRA system is achieved, for instance, it will expand the natural self-interest constituency by making IRAs more attractive to more people. This wider constituency will then be better able to achieve further extensions that in turn will further expand the constituency. This self-generating process in the private sector is identical to the political process that has forced programs in the public sector to grow and serve ever larger constituencies.

The business community, and financial institutions in particular, would be an obvious element in the constituency. Not only does business have a great deal to gain from a reform effort designed to stimulate private savings, but it also has the power to be politically influential and to be instrumental in mounting a public education campaign. This influence was clearly demonstrated in the fight to repeal withholding on interest and dividend income. The banking industry's ability to lobby and garner support for the repeal effort led many in Congress to reverse their earlier votes. Financial institutions, likewise, have been extremely effective in marketing various types of savings plans, such as All-Savers Certificates and IRAs, thereby building up public acceptance of these innovations.

165

Interest groups concerned with social security reform can be divided into the young, the middle-age working population, and the retired or those nearing retirement. Of these, the young are the most obvious constituency for reform and a natural ally for the private alternative. The overwhelming majority of people in this group have stated repeatedly that they have little or no confidence in the present social security system. Discontent will only grow as the taxes needed to support the system continue to rise and as the prospects for a reasonable return on one's "contribution" continue to fade.

Despite misgivings about social security, however, the young have yet to have a significant impact on the political process as it relates to reform measures. It is imperative, therefore, that they be informed about the problems inherent in the current system and that they be organized behind the private alternative.

Clearly, an important thread running through the entire strategy is education. An education campaign is needed to gain the support of key individuals in the media as well as to win over vital constituencies for political reform. The banking industry and other business groups that can benefit from expanded IRAs must be encouraged to play a central role in educating the public about the benefits of the private plan. They can do this both through their commercial advertising and through public relations.

Weakening the Opposition

Individual Accounts

To emphasize how unfavorably social security compares with the private alternative, the Social Security Administration should be required to establish an individual account for each person participating in the program. Furthermore, each person should be provided with an annual statement showing how much he has paid into the system and what benefits he can expect to receive. Individuals could then compare their returns from private investment with their returns under social security. Such a scheme would illustrate in cold numbers just what the program means for different individuals, and would help reveal the inter- and intragenerational distribution that occurs under the current system. The retired population might then come to realize that they have not purchased an earned annuity but instead are receiving a tremendous welfare subsidy. Younger workers, on the other hand, would see just how much of

166

a loss they are taking by participating in the program. This mechanism for demonstrating the individual gains and losses that occur under social security is a key step in weakening public support for the present system.[7]

The technology for creating a reporting system already exists. Using it simply requires an improvement in the computer system of the Social Security Administration. The SSA, however, undoubtedly would claim that the enormous cost and complexity of such a system would prevent it from providing what would be highly embarrassing information. Fortunately, there are private-sector companies, such as Accucomp Financial Services, that are willing to compile the necessary information from an employee's tax returns for a very modest fee. (Accucomp does it for $35.)[8] The SSA could be required to contract out the service to such companies, or taxpayers could receive a tax credit for arranging it themselves.

Detaching Supporters of Social Security

The final element of the strategy must be to propose moving to a private social security system in such a way as to detach, or at least neutralize, segments of the coalition that supports the existing system. A necessary step toward this objective is to honor all outstanding claims on the current system. Without such a commitment, we can never overcome the political opposition to reform because the retired (or nearly retired) population will continue to strongly oppose any package that threatens to significantly reduce their benefits. Retaining the obligation to fund existing liabilities, however, will necessarily place constraints on the mechanisms that can be used to move the country toward a private system.

The problem of implementing a private system makes the British model particularly attractive. It is clear, in Britain at least, that workers are quite prepared to make some payments into social security even though they will not receive benefits, provided they acquire the right to escape from a governmentally operated retire-

---

[7]Anthony Pellechio and Gordon Goodfellow have calculated these in "Individual Gains and Losses from Social Security before and after the 1983 Amendments," *Cato Journal* 3 (Fall 1983): 417–42.

[8]See Accucomp's ad in the 1983 edition of *Money Guide,* published by the editors of *Money,* p. 61.

ment system in which they have little confidence. We should consider, therefore, modifying Peter Ferrara's phase-in plan.[9]

Under Ferrara's plan, workers would be allowed to invest part, and eventually all, of the money they now pay into social security in expanded IRAs, in return for a corresponding reduction in their future social security benefits. Under our proposed modification, workers who choose to opt out of the system would not only lose their corresponding future benfits but would even have them reduced somewhat further for the privilege of getting out of social security. This added reduction in benefits could be viewed as a tax that would be used to pay off the system's remaining obligations.

An interim "opting-out tax" hardly conforms with the principles of fairness; yet it makes good political sense. If the support for leaving social security is as great as it seems, then it is unlikely that the level of contracting out will be significantly reduced by requiring workers to make some payment into the system while they withdraw and lose benefits (assuming, for the sake of argument, that they ever would have received those benefits!). But the opting-out tax would have important political advantages. It would serve to calm the fears of the elderly because the net phase-out losses to the social security fund would be smaller under opting out than under the Ferrara plan, for virtually the same reduction in future liabilities. Hence, under an opting-out plan the support needed from general revenues would be smaller, and the threat to the trust funds would be reduced.

This modification would slightly dampen the enthusiasm of young workers, who are a strong segment of the coalition for change. But on the other hand, this modification would help to meet the concerns of the elderly and of the taxpayers and beneficiaries of federal programs who might resist the use of general revenues to cover the phase-in period.

Detaching workers who have made substantial tax payments into social security may not prove to be too difficult. A number of proposals have been put forward in which the worker's accumulated "contributions," plus interest, would be given to him in the form of an interest-bearing bond, payable at retirement.[10] This bond would have a market value and could be sold, with the proceeds

[9]We refer specifically to Ferrara's "family security plan," as discussed in *The Family [Security] Plan*, pp. 49–73.

[10]See Ferrara, *The Inherent Contradiction*, pp. 340–50.

to be invested in a tax-deductible IRA. An appropriate version of this proposal should make it possible to gain some support even from those who have a substantial stake in the current system.

Conclusion

The last few years have demonstrated beyond a doubt that social security can be reformed only by treating the issue primarily as a political problem. There is little point in arguing over the nuances of theoretical plans if the political dynamics are not altered; no amount of logic will overcome an unfavorable coalition of interest groups.

It is also clear that the strategy we adopt must be flexible. It would be self-defeating to lay down a rigid blueprint and blindly adhere to it. Indeed, we must be prepared to refine segments of the plan, such as the opting-out mechanism or the design of the super IRA, to meet the changing political circumstances.

Finally, we must be prepared for a long campaign. The next social security crisis may be further away than many people believe. Or perhaps it will occur before the reform coalition is strong enough to achieve a political breakthrough. In either case, it could be many years before the conditions are such that a radical reform of social security is possible. But then, as Lenin well knew, to be a successful revolutionary, one must also be patient and consistently plan for real reform.

In the following chapter, the editor addresses some theoretical implications of shifting from a public pay-as-you-go system, like social security, to a private fully funded system. The issues raised in Carolyn Weaver's paper regarding the conventional pay-as-you-go analysis are further discussed here.

X. Social Security Reform: Some Theoretical Considerations

Peter J. Ferrara

One may agree that a private fully funded system of retirement support would be far superior to a public pay-as-you-go system such as social security. But that still leaves the question of whether it is *feasible* to make the transition from the current system to a private fully funded one. This transition issue will be examined in this chapter.

Social security, as has been noted, operates on a pay-as-you-go basis, with the funds paid into the system by today's workers not saved for their future benefits, but immediately paid out to finance the benefits of today's retirees. The benefits of today's workers are to be paid out of the taxes of the next generation of workers. Under a fully funded system, by contrast, the funds paid into the system by today's workers are saved for their own retirement. The benefits of current retirees would be paid out of funds similarly saved during their working years.

Some, most particularly Stanford University economist Michael Boskin, vociferously insist that shifting from social security's pay-as-you-go system to a private fully funded system will never be politically feasible because of a so-called double-payment problem.[1] They contend that the generation working during the time of transition would have to pay for two retirements, by paying for its own through the private system, while continuing to pay benefits to those already retired on social security, who have no saved funds in the current pay-as-you-go system with which to finance their benefits. But this argument and the double-payment label inaccurately characterize the nature and costs of such a transition.

There is in fact a clear transition cost to such a reform only to the extent

---

[1]See, for example, Michael T. Boskin, "Alternative Social Security Reform Proposals," statement prepared for the National Commission on Social Security Reform, August 20, 1982.

that the reform involves an increase in savings, and that is the same cost involved in any savings increase. Suppose starting next year workers were allowed to withdraw $20 billion in social security taxes annually to save in their Individual Retirement Accounts (IRAs) for part of their retirement benefits. The future social security benefits of these workers would be reduced proportionally to the reduction in their social security taxes, but the benefits of today's elderly would continue to be paid in full. The loss in revenue to pay the benefits of the currently retired would be equal to the increased savings in the IRAs. If the government simply increased its borrowing to cover this revenue loss and pay the benefits of today's elderly, there would be no net loss—or increase—in savings. At the same time, there would be no increased financial burden on the current working generation to pay for "two retirements."

If, however, the government covered the $20 billion revenue loss in this example by raising taxes or cutting other government expenditures, rather than by increasing borrowing, there would be a $20 billion increase in savings. The cost of this savings increase would be $20 billion in reduced present consumption due to increased taxes or reduced spending. *But this very same cost would be involved in any $20 billion increase in savings, no matter how it came about: any $20 billion increase in savings must, by definition, entail a $20 billion reduction in present consumption.* The commitment to continue paying the full benefits of the elderly means only that the reduced consumption would not come out of social security benefits. But that is almost surely true of any other savings increase as well.[2]

This savings increase, moreover, brings the same full long-term returns and increases in production as any other savings increase. That is, the new $20 billion in increased savings invested through IRAs would generate increased production equal to the full before-tax rate of return on capital just like any other invested savings.

This analysis indicates that the desirability of such reform, to the extent that it involves any associated transition cost and attendant savings increase, must be evaluated the same way as the desirability of any other savings increase: the short-term sacrifice must be weighed against the long-term

[2]Those who argue that social security expenditures should be reduced in order to reduce the government's deficit and thereby increase savings are arguing that the reduced consumption entailed by a savings increase should in fact come from reduced social security benefits. This approach appears to run directly contrary to widely held public opinion and may be the most painful way to increase savings.

174

returns. One cannot determine a priori that such a tradeoff, inherent in every savings increase, would necessarily be perceived as a bad deal. The desirability of this cost/benefit tradeoff depends on the subjective preferences of workers, which cannot be scientifically prejudged. One can determine the reform's desirability only by putting it up for a vote and by campaigning for or against it based on one's preferences, weighing all of its benefits against its costs.

Perhaps this can be made more clear by pointing out that shifting from a public pay-as-you-go system to a *private* fully funded system is no different in regard to the issues just discussed than shifting from a public pay-as-you-go system to a *public* fully funded system, that is, to fully funded social security. All else being equal, accumulating full reserves for social security surely involves a sharp increase in savings, along with higher costs for current workers, who contribute the increased revenues. But clearly, one cannot determine a priori that fully funding social security would always necessarily appear to be a bad deal. It depends on how voters value the tradeoff between the short-term costs and increased returns of the system earned by the increased reserve assets (as well as the other long-term benefits of full funding).

Indeed, Harvard economist Martin Feldstein, former chairman of the president's Council of Economic Advisers, has argued for more than a decade that social security should be fully funded precisely because he believes the long-term benefits of full funding are so clearly worth the short-term costs.[3] Feldstein's position is directly contrary to the view of those who say that shifting to a private fully funded system will always appear unattractive. *If shifting to a public fully funded system is worth the transition costs, so is shifting to a private fully funded system.* In fact, there are many more

---

[3]See Martin S. Feldstein, "Toward a Reform of Social Security," *Public Interest* (Summer 1975); idem, "Facing the Social Security Crisis," Harvard Institute of Economic Research Discussion Paper no. 492 (Cambridge, Mass., July 1976); idem, "Social Insurance," Harvard Institute of Economic Research Discussion Paper no. 477 (Cambridge, Mass., May 1976); idem, "The Optimal Financing of Social Security," Harvard Institute of Economic Research Discussion Paper no. 388 (Cambridge, Mass., November 1974); idem, *Strengthening Social Security, Testimony before the House Ways and Means Committee,* May 15, 1977; and idem, *Summary of Testimony on Social Security,* Subcommittee on Fiscal Policy, Joint Economic Committee, May 27, 1976.

advantages to shifting to a private-sector system, which should make it even more worthwhile.[4]

One can determine a priori that shifting to a private fully funded system is necessarily well worth the costs if one accepts as given the widely held proposition that the U.S. economy is not now producing an adequate, optimum level of savings and, therefore, that a savings increase sufficient to eliminate this inadequacy is well worth the costs.[5] One may accept such a proposition out of a belief that social security itself has drastically reduced national savings as workers reduce the amount of retirement savings they would otherwise accumulate, due to this reliance on social security, which produces no offsetting savings.[6] Or one may hold that government taxes, regulations, deficits, or other policies have reduced savings below the level workers would choose in a truly free market.

Whatever the reason, if one believes that a sharp savings increase is warranted and well worth the costs, then it follows that shifting from social security to a private fully funded system is necessarily also well worth the costs (as long as the resulting savings increase is not more than that deemed warranted, which is unlikely since any such increase can be so easily reduced). Through such reform, whatever savings increase results is produced with the same costs

[4]For a discussion of these advantages, see Peter J. Ferrara, *Social Security: The Inherent Contradiction* (Washington: Cato Institute, 1980); and idem, *Social Security Reform: The Family [Security] Plan* (Washington: Heritage Foundation, 1982).

[5]It is not contended here that this proposition is necessarily correct, but only that those who accept it must necessarily find the reform worthwhile.

It is also not contended here that a shortfall of savings produced by some government intervention should be offset by another government intervention to increase savings (the proper policy instead being to eliminate the original government intervention). The reform does not involve a new government intervention into the private marketplace, but rather the privatization of a public program.

Moreover, the purpose of the reform is not to increase savings. The purpose is to shift the functions of social security to the private sector as much as possible. Incidentally among the advantages of such reform, however, are the benefits of any savings increase that may be necessarily involved in such reform. These benefits must be weighed together with the other benefits of the reform in deciding whether it should be adopted.

It is also not contended here that the reform would produce any particular level of savings increase, or necessarily any savings increase at all. If there is no savings increase involved in the reform, however, there is no special transition cost for the initial working generation, and the reform still seems clearly worthwhile.

[6]For further discussion of social security's impact on savings, see chapter 4 of this volume and Ferrara, *The Inherent Contradiction*, chap. 3.

and benefits as any other savings increase of the same magnitude. Moreover, the reform provides at no extra cost the many other benefits that result from performing the functions of social security through the private sector.[7] The reform would thus be the best and most beneficial method of producing any such savings increase deemed warranted.

The purpose here, however, is not to attempt to demonstrate a priori that shifting to a private fully funded system is necessarily worth the costs. Rather, it is simply to demonstrate that one cannot determine a priori that such reform would necessarily appear *not* to be worth the costs. This leaves such reform open to debate, ultimately subject to decision based on the subjective value preferences of voters.

There is, admittedly, a special complication in this analysis with regard to the first working generation at the time such reform is adopted. This generation, by paying the benefits of the elderly as noted above, would under the current system have become entitled to full social security benefits itself. But in shifting to the private fully funded system, these workers would have to give up social security benefits and rely on the benefits of the private system instead. The following generation of workers would be saving for their own benefits through the private system, rather than paying the social security benefits of the prior generation.

The forgoing of benefits by the initial working generation does not change the costs or benefits of the reform in the aggregate. The forgone benefits result merely from the elimination of a redistribution between two generations—the working generation at the time of reform and the following generation—a redistribution rendered unnecessary by the retirement benefits of the new private system. The elimination of this redistribution does not reduce the benefits of any savings increase resulting from the reform. The increased production from any such increase would still be the same as that from any other savings increase of the same magnitude. Because the aggregate costs and benefits of the reform remain the same, the elimination of this redistribution should not change the appraisal from a neutral perspective as to whether the reform's costs would be worth its benefits.

Nevertheless, the elimination of this redistribution—in effect a cost of the reform to the initial working generation—raises an

---

[7]For references to a discussion of these benefits, see footnote 4.

important political question: would subtracting the value of these forgone social security benefits from the overall benefits of the reform necessarily make the reform unattractive to the initial working generation, given whatever transition cost, if any, it would have to bear? This question is crucial politically because the initial working generation includes most voters at any particular time. The future generations that would benefit from eliminating the unnecessary redistribution will never be able to vote on the issue.

Despite the loss of this redistribution, one still cannot determine a priori that the initial working generation would necessarily find the reform unattractive. One key reason is the fact that the private retirement benefits would be so much higher than the social security benefits promised to those entering the work force today and in the future that forgoing social security benefits would affect only a small fraction of the private benefits. To see this clearly, we must examine the returns that would be earned on payments into the private system.

As noted in chapter 1, studies by Martin Feldstein and others indicate that the before-tax real rate of return on private capital investment in the American economy is at least 12 percent.[8] This figure is not meant to represent, and does not represent, the returns routinely available to average investors, but it is the appropriate measure for our discussion here, for it represents the full amount of benefits that would be produced by payments into the private fully funded system (since such payments, of course, would be

---

[8]Martin Feldstein, "National Saving in the United States," Harvard Institute of Economic Research Discussion Paper no. 506 (Cambridge, Mass., October 1976); idem, "Toward a Reform of Social Security," *Public Interest* (Summer 1975): 75–95; idem, "The Optimal Financing of Social Security," Harvard Institute of Economic Research Discussion Paper no. 388 (Cambridge, Mass., November 1974). Studies by others have found returns in about the same range. See J. A. Stockfish, "Measuring the Social Rate of Return on Private Investment," in *Discounting for Time and Risk in Energy Policy*, ed. Robert C. Lind (Washington: Resources for the Future, 1982); D. M. Holland and S. Myers, "Trends in Corporate Profitability and Capital Costs," in *The Nation's Capital Needs*, ed. R. Lindsay (New York: Committee for Economic Development, 1979), pp. 103–89; W. D. Nordhaus, "The Falling Share of Profits," *Brookings Papers on Economic Activity*, vol. 2 (Washington: Brookings Institution, 1974), pp. 169–208; J. A. Gorman, "Nonfinancial Corporations: New Measures of Output and Input," *Survey of Current Business* (March 1974); J. A. Stockfish, *The Planning-Programming-Budgeting System: Progress and Potentials, Hearings before the Subcommittee on Economy in Government*, Joint Economic Committee (Washington: Government Printing Office, September 1967), pp. 133–43.

saved and held in the form of private capital investments). As discussed in chapter 1, all of these benefits would be enjoyed by the initial working generation at the time of the reform in one form or another. Through taxation of these returns, the government would merely be appropriating part of these benefits for other uses. These increased resources available to the government would go to provide either government services or reductions in other taxes. Either way, individuals would still be receiving the full before-tax benefits of the private system. The social security returns discussed below are the full untaxed returns provided by the program as well.

Moreover, investors do not directly receive this full return in the economy today primarily because of the high taxes at the corporate and personal levels that must be paid on investment returns.[9] Also, many private savings vehicles transfer much of the risk of investment to other persons or institutions in return for lower yield. But since the full return through the private fully funded system represents newly created income that would not exist at all if the current social security system simply continued without change, the government cannot now be planning on receiving as revenue any portion of this new, unexpected income to finance currently planned government activities. Consequently, the government could allow the total return on retirement investments in a new, private fully funded system to remain completely untaxed and devoted by the generation working at the time of the reform entirely to its private retirement benefits. Moreover, risk could be thoroughly minimized without sacrificing this return (since it is already an average return on all equity capital) by pooling and diversifying equity investments through such simple and universally available vehicles as broad-based mutual funds, which are particularly suitable for long-term retirement investments.

In the discussion that follows, we will, therefore, consider the retirement benefits workers could receive under the private fully funded system in comparison with social security as if they were allowed to keep the entire before-tax return on capital investments made through the private retirement system. This will allow the

[9]This includes not only taxes on net income or profits, but also the many taxes that must be paid regardless of profits, such as the social security payroll tax itself, unemployment insurance taxes, sales taxes, property taxes, and many others. Investments made through today's Individual Retirement Accounts (IRAs) are certainly far from entirely exempt from such taxes.

most direct comparison of the full benefits available under the private fully funded system with the full benefits available under social security. We will also consider the benefits available under the private system in comparison with social security in the case where some of the private returns are taxed away, of course counting the new tax revenues generated by the private system as part of its overall benefits.

The full 12 percent private-system return compares with a real return through social security for most young people entering the work force today of around 1 percent, and in many cases zero or even negative.[10] If returns through the private system were entirely untaxed, and the private system's investments regularly earned the full 12 percent, then most workers entering the work force today would receive benefits through the private system at least 20 times greater than those currently promised by social security.[11] Now, let us assume that as part of the reform the initial working generation itself would pay all remaining social security benefits to the current elderly through taxes, without borrowing.[12] The reform would present these workers with the question of whether they would find it worthwhile to pay an additional 1 times social security taxes into the private system, beyond paying for the present elderly, with a net return from the private system of, in effect, 20 times social security's promised benefits minus 1 times those benefits.

In actuality, of course, retired workers would enjoy benefits a full 20 times those promised through social security if they opted for the private system under the assumptions and circumstances outlined above. Since they are already paying 1 times social security taxes for 1 times social security benefits under the current system, what they would receive at the margin for the additional 1 times social security taxes paid into the private system is an additional 19 times social security benefits. The 1 further times social security benefits they actually receive should properly be attributed to the

[10]See discussion in chapter 1.

[11]If one invests a certain sum each year in a system paying a 12 percent annual real return, and invests an equal sum each year in a system paying a 1.5 percent annual real return, after 15 years the total accumulated through the first system would be more than 20 times greater than the total accumulated through the second system.

[12]All else being equal, this would increase savings by the maximum amount possible under such reform—the full amount these workers would pay into and save in the private system each year—as no savings would be offset by borrowing.

1 times social security taxes they must pay regardless of whether they choose the private system. Stated differently, the question offered by the reform is whether the initial generation of workers would find it attractive to trade the current system, in which they pay 1 times social security taxes for 1 times social security benefits, for a new system in which they would pay 2 times social security taxes for 20 times social security benefits.

Clearly, such a reform proposal could not be accurately described as asking workers to "pay twice for their retirement." Under the reform, workers would be asked to pay more, but they would receive much more as well. There is surely no means by which one can determine a priori that these workers would necessarily find this offer to be a bad deal, despite the fact that they would, in the process, lose a redistribution of 1 times social security benefits from the next generation. This loss would obviously be quite small relative to the overall benefits of the reform and consequently unlikely to make the difference in itself when workers judge whether the reform is desirable. The loss of this redistribution could be perceived as in effect a tax on the investment returns of the otherwise untaxed private retirement system, quite a small "tax" relative to the huge tax burdens regularly applicable to private investment returns. Workers do not have any such lightly taxed investment opportunity available to them today that might enable one to determine whether they would find it attractive.

Moreover, adjustments could be made that might make the reform even more attractive to the initial working generation. Because the benefits through the private system are potentially so high, workers and their employers could be allowed to save less each year for retirement through the private system than they would be required to pay into social security. They could, for example, be required to pay into the private system only one-half the amount they would be mandated to pay into social security. At a 12 percent real return, this would earn most workers at least 10 times the retirement benefits currently promised by social security.[13] Again assuming that the initial generation itself pays the remaining social security benefits to the elderly through its taxes, without borrowing, the issue becomes whether workers would perceive as worthwhile their

[13]If one invests a certain sum each year in a system earning a 1.5 percent annual real return, then after 45 years the total accumulated in the second would be at least 10 times the total accumulated in the first.

paying an additional one-half social security taxes into the private system, beyond paying for the present elderly, with a return from the private system of in effect 10 times the benefits promised by social security minus 1 times such benefits. Or, stated differently, the issue is whether the initial generation of workers would find it attractive to trade the current system, in which they pay 1 times social security taxes for 1 times social security benefits, for a new system in which they would pay one-and-a-half times social security taxes for 10 times social security benefits.

Another alternative is for the government to tax directly some of the investment returns from the private retirement system and use the new revenues to finance a portion of the remaining social security obligations to the elderly. Assuming that workers and their employers would be required to pay the same amounts into the private system that they are required to pay into social security, taxing away a third of the investment returns each year would finance roughly half of the remaining social security benefits,[14] an amount equal to about half the required payments into the private system.[15] At the same time, workers would still receive at least 7 times the retirement benefits promised by social security.[16] Since workers in the initial working generation would consequently be relieved of an obligation equal to half their private retirement payments through the returns of the private system, the cost of that

[14]If the amount to be paid into social security was instead paid into the private system with one-third of the before-tax return taxed away to pay social security benefits, then after 16 years there would be enough tax money generated each year to fund social security benefits completely. The tax funds would, therefore, pay more than half of the initial working generation's liability to the elderly over the generation's entire 40-years-plus work span.

[15]We may assume that 1 times social security taxes for this generation would be equal to the social security benefits it must pay to the elderly, since the program operates on a pay-as-you-go basis. So financing one-half such benefits to the elderly by taxation of the private system's returns finances an amount equal to one-half social security taxes for this generation. Since we are assuming here that these workers would be required to pay into social security, the amount of such benefits financed by taxation of the private returns would also be equal to one-half the payments into the private system.

[16]With one-third of the full 12 percent return taxed away, workers would receive an after-tax return of 8 percent on their retirement investments. If one invests a certain sum each year in a system paying an 8 percent annual real return, and invests an equal sum each year in a system paying a 1.5 percent annual real return, after 45 years the total accumulated through the first system would be 7 times greater than the total accumulated through the second system.

182

system would in effect be cut in half. With the initial generation of workers again paying remaining social security benefits through other taxes, without borrowing, the issue becomes whether these workers would perceive as desirable their paying an additional one-half social security taxes into the private system, beyond paying for the present elderly, with an effective return of 7 times social security benefits minus 1 times those benefits.[17] Or, again stated differently, the issue is whether the initial generation of workers would find it attractive to trade the current system, in which they pay 1 times social security taxes for 1 times social security benefits, for a new system in which they would pay one-and-a-half times social security taxes for 7 times social security benefits. Pragmatically, this might well be the alternative most likely to be offered workers through the reform, due to the practical difficulty of attempting to make the private system's investment returns entirely tax-exempt.[18]

If this would not be lucrative enough, it could be made still more so. The government could raise part of the funds needed to pay benefits promised to today's elderly by borrowing. The first working generation would therefore not have to finance this portion of social security benefits by reducing present consumption. Of course, such borrowing would partially reduce the savings increase produced by the reform, but there would be room for a substantial amount of borrowing while still maintaining a large savings increase. The borrowing could be paid off by the next working generation or by later generations, at which time their savings would increase.

With taxation of the private system's returns financing half the remaining obligations to the elderly (as described above), half of what would be left (one-fourth of the total) could, for example, be financed by borrowing. This would in effect relieve workers of obligations equal to an additional one-fourth of their payments into the private system, reducing the net additional cost of the private system over what workers would otherwise pay into social security

[17]The amount of private benefits workers receive here is less than under the alternative discussed above, in which workers pay half of social security taxes into the private system, because here the taxed-away portion of the returns each year is not left in the private system to earn further returns itself in future years.

[18]While practical difficulties exist in trying to make specific investments exempt from all taxes, a reformed Individual Retirement Account that would provide for such complete tax exemption has been proposed. See Ferrara, *The Inherent Contradiction*, chap. 11.

to one-fourth social security taxes.[19] The issue then becomes whether workers would find it worthwhile to pay this additional one-fourth social security taxes into the private system in exchange for a return on such payments of 7 times social security benefits minus 1 times those benefits.[20] Or, again stated differently, the issue is whether workers would find it attractive to trade the current system, in which they pay 1 times social security taxes for 1 times social security benefits, for a new system in which they would pay one-and-one-fourth times social security taxes for 7 times social security benefits.

Ultimately, the initial working generation could continue to be paid some additional benefits from the next working generation in addition to receiving the private system's benefits. The next working generation, which would otherwise not have any pending social security obligations to finance, could be taxed, for example, one-half times social security taxes to finance an additional one-half times social security benefits for the retired initial working generation. This would in effect be a way of phasing in the new system over more than one generation. Of course, the next generation could be taxed only a fraction of 1 times social security taxes to finance such benefits, or else we would not be phasing out the old system for the new, but adding the new system on top of the old. In any event, it would seem silly to have to make such a redistribution on top of the already high private retirement benefits. This would suggest that such a redistribution would probably not be necessary to make the reform sufficiently attractive to the initial working generation.

Beyond the higher monetary returns offered by a shift to a private fully funded system, there are many other important benefits that also must be weighed by the initial working generation. To begin

[19]As indicated in footnote 13, we may assume that 1 times social security taxes for the initial working generation would be equal to the social security benefits they must pay to the elderly. Financing one-fourth of these benefits by borrowing consequently relieves those workers of an obligation equal to one-fourth social security taxes. Since we are assuming that these workers would be required to pay into the private system the same amount they would be required to pay into social security, such borrowing relieves them of an obligation equal to one-fourth of their payments into the private system.

[20]This assumes that the interest on the borrowed funds is paid off by borrowing as well. Since the much larger, full market returns earned on contributions into the private system are also saved, however, this borrowing would still leave a large net increase in savings.

184

with, the reform would greatly increase the freedom of the worker in fundamental and meaningful ways.[21] Workers under a private system could still be required to make some provision for their retirement and insurance contingencies, but they could also be allowed to choose and control the investment and insurance purchases they would make to satisfy these requirements. A private-sector system would also allow workers the flexibility to tailor individual packages of investments and insurance coverage to their own personal needs and circumstances. Workers would also have greater freedom to choose their own retirement age, without social security's penalties for choosing later retirement.

There should also be less uncertainty associated with private benefits, since they would be supported by a fully funded system rather than by social security's unstable pay-as-you-go system. Workers would be quite relieved to be rid of periodic social security collapses and current doubts about the system's long-term viability. As Carolyn Weaver points out, workers would not be concerned about forgoing social security benefits that they feel they are probably not going to get anyway.[22]

Workers are also likely to view the benefit structure of the private system as far more equitable than the haphazard, crazy-quilt benefit structure of social security. Two workers paying exactly the same taxes into social security over their entire careers can actually receive widely differing benefit amounts. In the private system, each worker would receive back what he paid, plus interest, on an actuarial basis.[23]

In addition, the reform is likely to have substantial positive effects on the nation's economy. Any increase in savings would have beneficial effects beyond merely the newly generated income represented by the returns on the private retirement investments. The

---

[21]For further discussion of this increased freedom, see Peter J. Ferrara, *Social Security: Averting the Crisis*, (Washington: Cato Institute, 1982), chaps. 4 and 9.

[22]See chapter 7. For further discussion of social security's financing difficulties, see *Comment* following chapter 2 of this volume and Ferrara, *The Inherent Contradiction*, chap. 5.

[23]The social security benefit structure includes many elements that tend to provide a lower return for the poor, blacks, and other minorities than for other taxpayers. The lower life expectancy of these groups itself results in lower returns for these workers, since they on average live fewer years in retirement to collect benefits. For further discussion of these inequities, see Ferrara, *The Inherent Contradiction*, chap. 6.

more rapid economic growth induced by such an increase would reverberate throughout the economy, likely stimulating further economic growth in a supply-side boom. The new savings would also result in the creation of new jobs and increased employment. The reduction and eventual elimination of the payroll tax, made possible by the reform, would also help create new jobs and stimulate higher economic growth.[24]

Many in the initial working generation would be likely to consider the opportunity to work in a healthy and growing economy now to be an important substantive benefit of the reform. Unemployed workers who believed they would be able to get jobs as a result of the reform would probably find it well worthwhile, as would workers who believed that the reform would open up opportunities for better jobs. Similarly, fledgling or struggling entrepreneurs, as well as owners of established businesses, who believed that the reform would provide an improved economic climate for their enterprises would also quite likely favor it.

Many would also value highly the particularly important benefits of the reform for the poor. It is they who are most in need of the higher retirement benefits and improved economic opportunities that would result from the reform. It is also they who are least able to protect themselves from the uncertainties and inequities of the current system. The personal wealth each worker would accumulate through the private system would provide special opportunities for the poor to break out of the cycle of poverty by giving them control over some capital. Low-income workers would also be the ones to benefit most from any eventual reduction or elimination of the regressive payroll tax, which the reform would make possible.[25]

Special value would be seen by many also in the fact that with each worker accumulating substantial assets under his personal ownership through the private retirement system, total national wealth would be distributed far more equally. The concentration of national wealth could, as a result, be reduced by as much as a third.[26]

[24]For further discussion of these issues, see ibid., chap. 3.

[25]For further discussion of the impact of such reform on the poor, see ibid., chaps. 6 and 11.

[26]See Martin Feldstein, "Social Security and the Distribution of Wealth," *Journal of the American Statistical Association* (November 1976). For further discussion of this issue, see Ferrara, *The Inherent Contradiction*, chap. 6.

Those who favor limited government and reliance on free markets would find special value in the reform, as it would in effect "denationalize" the large portion of the pension and insurance industries now represented by social security, producing a major shift of economic functions from the public sector to the private sector. Federal spending, as a result, would be reduced by 25–30 percent, and this would also be prized by many.[27]

Those in the initial working generation may also be expected to take into account the benefits of the reform for their children, and many would also value its benefits for future generations and for society as a whole. If people are convinced that it makes much more sense to have a private system rather than social security, they will be willing to incur some costs over their lifetimes to set things right for the future.

Besides all these additional benefits, there would be still other important sources of cost savings during the transition to the private system. The loss of tax revenue resulting from workers' paying into the private system instead of social security might induce the government to close the revenue gap partially by cutting wasteful, unnecessary government spending that would not otherwise be cut.[28] Or it might at the very least induce the government to restrain the growth of wasteful spending. This elimination of waste would offset the cost of the reform for the first working generation.

The reform itself would directly eliminate some current waste. Shifting from social security to a private system would mean that the portion of social security benefits in effect constituting welfare assistance would instead be paid only through other, means-tested government programs, as the private system would not pay any such redistribution benefits. This would eliminate the current waste of welfare benefits paid through social security to many who are not poor, which occurs because the program has no means test.[29] Further cost savings would result simply from the efficiencies of the private market that would supplant social security. For example,

[27]Social security as a whole currently amounts to about 30 percent of the entire federal budget. If the insurance functions of the program were performed in the private sector, the great majority of this spending, if not virtually all of it, would on net be transferred to the private sector.

[28]This may, and probably preferably should, be a loss of income tax revenues. See chapter 11.

[29]For further discussion of this problem, see Ferrara, *The Inherent Contradiction*, chaps. 6 and 11.

disability incidence would probably be policed far more diligently by private, competitive insurance companies anxious to keep costs down.

The loss in tax revenues resulting from the reform might also induce the federal government to sell off assets it might otherwise keep unnecessarily, such as privately used government lands in the western United States. The proceeds from those sales could then be used to finance part of the benefits still owed the elderly generation at the time of the reform, so that such benefits would not have to be financed out of the present consumption of the initial working generation. Such assets would also likely be far more productive in the private sector, and the resulting increase in production would further offset the cost of the reform.

Finally, it must be recognized that the votes of only a majority of the initial working generation are necessary to approve the reform. Those especially sensitive to the above-described advantages of the reform would form the foundation of a pro-reform coalition. It is easy to see, for example, that those ideologically inclined to favor private markets and economic freedom would readily embrace such reform. Moreover, as seen in chapter 1, substantial segments of society are offered especially low returns by social security today, and those segments would also be particularly disposed toward joining a pro-reform coalition. Banks, insurance companies, mutual fund companies, stockbrokers, and other financial institutions with major new business prospects as a result of the reform could also be expected to support it heavily. In addition, many might feel relatively immune to any transition costs of the reform. Many might feel that they have the political clout in any event to prevent any increase in their taxes or any cuts in government benefits crucial to them. These voters would also more readily support the reform. Such factors ease the formation of an ultimately successful political coalition in favor of the reform.

In summary, *this discussion should clearly establish that one cannot determine a priori that a shift from social security to a private fully funded system will always necessarily appear unattractive to the generation working at the time of the reform.* Such a reform would involve special short-term costs for this generation only to the extent that it would mean an increase in savings, and this cost would be the same for *any* increase in savings: forgone present consumption equal to the amount of savings increase. This cost must be weighed against the long-term benefits of the savings increase—again the same as for any other savings increase—and against the many other beneficial features of the reform. In simple financial terms, workers in the initial generation would pay more than under the current system, but they would also get much more, even while forgoing the redistribution from the next working generation that would otherwise occur through social security. There are also many benefits of the reform involving improved quality of service; increased freedom, security, and control; an improved economy now; improved prospects for the initial generation's children and for future generations; as well as many ideologically perceived advantages.

With this constellation of costs and benefits, it would be silly to suggest that isolated academics can determine a priori that a majority coalition can never be built in favor of such reform. Whether the initial working generation would favor such reform depends on the subjective value preferences of the workers themselves regarding the reform's costs and benefits. Their appraisal can be determined only, if at all, by putting the measure up for a vote through candidates campaigning for or against it.

Of course, one can still develop a strong opinion based on personal judgment as to whether workers would find the reform attractive. The view here is that workers are likely to find the overall benefits of such reform overwhelming and easily worth the costs. The simplicity and attractiveness of the specific reform proposal offered in the next chapter should in fact spawn deep-seated enthusiasm over the prospects for real reform.[30]

[30]The above discussion should also make clear that the argument in favor of the reform is not that it would make the economy grow so fast as to eliminate any short-term costs on net, as has sometimes been erroneously suggested. Rather, the argument is that the short-term costs should be perceived as worth the long-term benefits, as will be further indicated in the next chapter.

A PROPOSAL FOR REFORM

XI. Social Security and the Super IRA: A Populist Proposal

Peter J. Ferrara

Fundamental reform to solve the problems of social security is possible if the reform is structured carefully to meet the concerns of the elderly and workers. The problems of the current system are so great, and consequently the potential benefits of reform so vast for virtually everyone, that properly structured reform could indeed be quite popular. The key to recognizing this is to understand precisely how reform can be structured to gain the overwhelming benefits of solving social security's woes for the elderly and workers in particular, while not harming any of their vital interests. The detailed mechanics of such reform are explained in this chapter.

Guaranteeing the Elderly

Social security is the first and foremost for the elderly. Consequently, for fundamental social security reform to have any chance of public acceptance, it must first demonstrate how it would secure the benefits of the elderly. Once the elderly are satisfied that their benefits are secure, then changes may be considered that would enable today's workers to have a secure and prosperous retirement as well. The first principle of reform must be, therefore, to reject benefit cuts as any part of the solution to the program's problems.

But more than merely rejecting benefit cuts is necessary. Those advancing fundamental social security reform should take the lead in trying to improve the legal status of social security benefits, so that such benefits would be guaranteed once a worker retires in reliance on them. The Supreme Court held in a 1960 decision, *Flemming* v. *Nestor*,[1] that retirees have no contractual right to their promised social security benefits despite their past payments into the system and that Congress has the power to reduce or cut off the program's benefits to any or all of the elderly at any time. As

[1]363 U.S. 610.

part of an overall fundamental social security reform package, Congress should make the statutory changes necessary to overturn this ruling and provide a firm guarantee for social security benefits.

Congress could do this by providing that at the time a worker retires in reliance on his future, promised social security benefits, he would receive a U.S. government bond stating his contractual entitlement to those benefits. All those already retired at the time of the reform would receive such a bond as well. The bond would not change the amount of the retiree's promised benefits in any way. It would simply embody a contract with the government promising that the retiree will receive his monthly benefit amount each month for the rest of his life, plus COLA increases, calculated under the law in effect at the time he retired (or, for those already retired when the reform is adopted, when the bond is received).

Congress would statutorily express its intent that the retiree would have the same legal status in regard to his social security benefits, as promised by his social security bond, as a U.S. Treasury bondholder has in regard to the payment of the interest and principal on his bond. The Constitution prohibits the federal government from reneging on the payment of interest and/or principal on any U.S. government bond. Similarly, under the proposed social security bond system, it would be unconstitutional to cut the expected social security benefits of workers once they retired. Congress would retain the authority to reduce benefits for new beneficiaries in the future.

This reform would produce a meaningful change in the security of the elderly. It would provide as firm a guarantee as is legally possible to assure the social security benefits of those already retired, a guarantee that has never been abrogated in the context of other U.S. government obligations.

The Super IRA

Besides the above-described social security bonds, further elements of an initial fundamental reform package would involve modifications of the existing Individual Retirement Account (IRA) system to create "Super IRAs."

One such modification would provide that starting on a certain date, say, January 1, 1986, workers would be allowed to contribute to their IRAs each year an amount up to 20 percent of their social security retirement taxes (OASI), in addition to any other amounts they may contribute under current law. Instead of the usual IRA income tax deduction for these contributions, however, workers would instead receive a dollar-for-dollar income tax credit equal to the amount of such contributions. Workers would also have the right to direct their employers to contribute up to 20 percent of the employer share of the tax to the workers' IRAs, with each employer again receiving a full income tax credit for these amounts.

Workers who utilized this tax credit option would then have their future social security benefits reduced to the extent they did so. A worker who opted for the full credit during his entire working career would have his social security benefits reduced by 20 percent, the maximum reduction. A worker who took half the credit each year would have his future benefits reduced by 10 percent. Workers could take the credit in some years and not others, and in differing degrees each year, with a formula to calculate the resulting proportional benefit reductions. Benefits would be reduced less under the formula the older a worker is when he takes the credit, since, with fewer years until retirement, there is less time for an older worker's IRA contribution to earn investment returns. In retirement, of course, the accumulated funds in the expanded, Super IRAs would pay benefits that would more than make up for the forgone social security benefits, leaving workers with higher retirement benefits overall.

Workers already in the work force when the reform is adopted would receive full credit toward their social security benefits for past taxes paid into the program. Past years would be treated simply as if the worker chose not to utilize the credit in those years. These workers would receive reduced social security benefits only for years in which they actually did utilize the credit.

The income tax credit is meant to be in effect a partial rebate of social security taxes to those who chose to substitute Super IRAs partially for social security. But it is crucially important to recognize that since the tax credit is taken against income taxes rather than payroll taxes, social security revenues would continue to flow into the program in full to finance benefits for today's elderly. The credit option would result only in a loss of income tax revenues, discussed further below.

Current IRA rights for workers would otherwise not be changed. Workers could forgo the tax-credit option entirely, making whatever IRA contributions they desired as allowed under current law and taking the current IRA income tax deduction for such contributions without any reduction in future social security benefits. Or workers could choose to make only IRA contributions for which they took the income tax credit instead of the current deduction. Or workers could contribute both the maximum allowed under current law, taking the deduction for such contributions, and the maximum for which they could take the credit.

Under this system, workers would naturally always have the right to forgo the Super IRAs altogether and remain entirely in social security as is, without penalty. Social security benefits for workers who chose to do so would not be reduced in any way under the reform.

An additional element of an initial reform package would expand the Super-IRA option further. Starting on a later date, say, January 1, 1990, workers would be allowed to contribute further amounts to their IRAs each year, up to 10 percent of the employee's OASI taxes, for the purchase of life insurance. Workers could also direct their employers to contribute up to this amount to the workers' IRAs for such purchases. Employer and employee would again each receive income tax credits equal to the amount of their contributions, instead of the usual IRA deduction.

An employee with no dependents who may not need such life insurance coverage would be allowed to devote these additional contributions to his retirement benefits instead. An employee with one dependent would be allowed to use half these contributions for retirement.

Social security currently pays survivors benefits on behalf of deceased taxpayers who leave dependent spouses and young children or who leave elderly spouses. For workers under 65, private life insurance can perform this function entirely. Consequently, the survivors benefits of a worker who died before 65 would be reduced to the extent that he had used the tax-credit option to purchase life insurance in force when he died. In all other respects, this tax-credit option would be the same as the first credit option discussed above.

Later legislation would expand this Super-IRA option further. The maximum income tax credit for IRA contributions could be increased to 40 percent of OASI taxes, for both employees and employers, in return for further future social security benefit reductions. Eventually this credit could be expanded to 100 percent of OASI taxes. Workers would then be allowed to purchase disability and retirement health insurance through their IRAs, with further income tax credits allowed for these purchases in return for reduced reliance on social security. Ultimately, workers would have the complete freedom to choose how much to rely on Super IRAs or social security.

But an initial fundamental reform package could be legislated with just the three elements discussed above: (1) the social security bond guaranteeing benefits to the elderly; (2) the income tax credit for Super-IRA contributions in return for reduced future social security retirement benefits, with the annual maximum on the credit equal to 20 percent of OASI taxes; and (3) the income tax credit for Super-IRA contributions for life insurance purchases to replace social security survivors insurance, with the annual maximum on the credit equal to 10 percent of OASI taxes.

The Cost of the Reform

The costs of the above-described initial reform package involve the income tax revenue losses that would result from utilization of the income tax credits. If the first income tax credit above (up to a maximum of 20 percent of OASI taxes for Super-IRA retirement benefit contributions) were in effect in the current fiscal year (FY 1985), and workers utilized it at twice the rate they currently utilize conventional IRAs, the income tax revenue loss for the year would be $14.5 billion.[2] If workers continued to utilize the credit at the same rate in future years, the income tax revenue loss would be of the same magnitude relative to the federal budget and the economy in those years as the $14.5 billion loss in FY 1985.

This loss would eventually be offset completely by reduced social security expenditures, as more and more workers retired relying to a large extent on Super IRAs rather than social security. Long before this point, however, the revenue loss would be eliminated on net, due to new revenues generated from the increased investment through the Super IRAs. The newly generated returns of IRA investments themselves would still be subject to the corporate income tax, social security payroll taxes, and other federal, state, and local taxes, without even considering any revenue increase due to any

[2]Calculated from the *1984 Annual Report of the Board of Trustees of the Federal Old-Age and Survivors Insurance and Disability Insurance Trust Funds* (Washington: Government Printing Office, April 5, 1984).

possible stimulative effects of the reform on the overall economy.[3]

Before the revenue loss was offset by these factors, moreover, there would be increased savings through the Super IRAs at least equal to the amount of revenue lost, since the credit would be allowed only for IRA savings.[4] So even if the government had to borrow entirely to cover the temporary revenue loss, there would be no net increase in the government borrowing drain on private savings.

Surely not everyone would start utilizing the Super-IRA option to the maximum from day one. Suggesting that twice the number of current IRA contributors, or 40 percent of all workers, would do so, as assumed above, is probably still optimistic. The above estimate of the initial revenue loss may consequently be on the high side. Over time, however, one could expect the percentage of workers choosing Super IRAs to increase steadily, until eventually the great majority of workers were doing so. This would tend to increase the revenue loss from the tax credits over time, but the reduced expenditures and increased tax revenues otherwise resulting from the reform would at the same time be developing considerable momentum, sharply mitigating any such increase. The temporary net revenue loss may, therefore, eventually increase somewhat for a few years from the levels indicated above, but it would of course

[3]Even with this tax burden on IRA investments, there would still be plenty of investment return left for the Super IRAs themselves to receive and accumulate the returns indicated in chapter 1. With before-tax real returns on capital at 12 percent (see discussion in chapters 1 and 10), if we assume 4 percentage points were taxed away, that would provide for a rapid buildup of revenues to offset the initial revenue loss resulting from the reform. Enough after-tax returns would then be left for the Super IRAs to receive the 6 percent return that was the focus of chapter 1, still leaving 2 percentage points for slippage.

[4]To avoid the danger of a mere shifting of existing savings into IRAs to obtain the credit, workers should be prohibited from withdrawing before retirement IRA contributions for which they obtained the credit, and the returns associated with those contributions. (These returns could be identified by requiring segregated accounting within the IRA for contributions for which the credit was taken.) This would make the IRA savings unsuitable as a substitute for nonretirement savings, since it could not be used for nonretirement purposes. Because social security benefits would be reduced for credited IRA contributions, the IRA savings would be needed to replace those lost benefits and therefore would not be available as a substitute for other retirement savings either. Any shifting of existing savings into IRAs rather than new savings to obtain the credit should therefore be negligible because such IRA savings would not be able to perform the function of other savings.

198

still be eliminated eventually due to the reduced expenditures and increased revenues otherwise resulting from the reform. In the interim, also, the reform would still produce increased savings to offset any need for the government to increase borrowing to cover the temporary revenue loss.

The second income tax credit discussed above (up to a maximum of 10 percent of OASI taxes for Super-IRA life insurance purchases) would be slated under the proposed package to begin on a later date than the first tax credit. But if it were in effect in FY 1985 and if workers utilized it twice as much as they utilize IRAs now, the income tax revenue loss for the year would be $7 billion. Social security expenditure reductions resulting from this credit to offset the revenue loss would accrue far more quickly than in the case of the first credit. The survivors of workers who died in the very first year while relying on insurance purchased through the credit would immediately receive private insurance benefits rather than social security benefits. After just a few years, as this continued, the revenue loss would be offset completely by reduced social security expenditures.

In addition, increased savings and investment would also result from this credit, as the amounts paid in life insurance premiums would generally be set aside in lump sums, held by either the beneficiary or the insurance company, to finance the stream of benefits to be paid on behalf of the deceased worker. This increased investment would again generate new tax revenues that, in conjunction with the reduced expenditures, would rapidly offset the revenue loss due to the credit. In the meantime, the increased savings would generally again offset any increased government borrowing to cover the temporary revenue loss.

The Benefits of the Reform

In return for these manageable, feasible costs, the benefits of the proposed Super-IRA reform would be compelling.

The security of the elderly would be greatly enhanced through the proposed social security bonds, which would create a contractual entitlement to promised social security benefits and in effect make it unconstitutional to cut the benefits of people once they retire. The reform would not reduce benefits to the elderly in any way.

Social security itself would be greatly strengthened by the reform, enhancing the ability of the program to pay promised benefits. This is because while the program's payroll tax revenues would be maintained in full, the program's expenditures in the future would be reduced substantially as workers relied more and more on Super IRAs rather than social security. As a result, likely long-term deficits in the program would be sharply reduced. If the Super-IRA option were expanded rapidly enough, the long-term financing problems of the program (even under the most pessimistic projections) would be eliminated entirely. Indeed, with the Super-IRA option eventually expanded to the maximum, social security expenditures would likely be reduced dramatically, allowing room for sharp reductions in payroll taxes.

In addition, workers who desired would have complete freedom to remain entirely in social security as is, without penalty, forgoing the Super-IRA option altogether. Those already in the work force who opted for the Super IRAs to whatever degree would receive full credit toward social security benefits for amounts they paid into the program in the past or might pay in the future.

Those workers who did opt for the Super IRAs could expect much higher retirement benefits. As indicated in chapter 1, with a fully expanded Super-IRA option most young workers entering the work force today could expect at full market returns to receive through Super IRAs three to five times the benefits promised by social security. Even career minimum-wage earners could expect more than twice the benefits. Eventually, the amounts workers would be mandated to pay into the Super IRAs could be reduced, since workers need not be required to have such high retirement incomes. This would allow workers more disposable income over their working years.

The Super-IRA benefits, moreover, would be financed on a fully funded basis, securing them against the financing problems inherent in social security's current pay-as-you-go system. Workers would no longer be plagued with the periodic financial collapses of social security. Simple, universally available investments that minimize risk could be readily purchased by workers through their Super IRAs. For example, as indicated in chapter 1, workers could purchase shares in very broad-based pools of stocks, such as mutual funds, in a sense buying a piece of the economy as a whole.[5] Workers would then bear no greater risk than the chance of collapse of the entire economy, a risk faced by social security as well. Work-

[5]Such an investment would yield the returns considered in chapter 1.

ers could also choose to invest their Super-IRA funds in any of a number of government-guaranteed investments, such as U.S. government bonds, although such investments would likely yield lower returns than broad-based stockholdings.

The reform would also allow workers much greater freedom of choice and control over their own incomes. While workers would still be required to provide for their retirement and insurance contingencies, through the Super IRAs they would be able to choose and control the investment and insurance vehicles to satisfy these requirements. Each worker would consequently be able to tailor his own individual package of investments and insurance coverage to suit his personal needs and circumstances. With workers directly and personally owning and controlling their Super-IRA funds as private property, their retirement prospects would not be subject to the same politicization and vagaries of public support as with social security.

The Super IRAs would also allow workers complete freedom to choose their retirement age after the 59-1/2 minimum age for IRA benefits under current law. Workers would not lose benefits for choosing late retirement, as is the case with social security. Workers could also choose to leave some of their Super-IRA funds to their heirs, which they cannot do with social security. Super IRAs in addition would offer workers instantaneous vesting and complete portability. The worker's ownership rights to Super-IRA funds would vest as soon as they were paid into his account, and the worker would retain these property rights no matter how often he changed jobs or where he went to work.

Benefits paid through the Super IRAs would also be completely equitable, with each worker receiving back in benefits what he paid in contributions, plus interest, on an actuarial basis. This would allow workers to avoid the inequities of the current social security benefit structure, in which workers do not receive equal benefits for past taxes paid into the program. For example, larger benefits are paid to workers with nonworking spouses or with dependent children, even though these workers may have exactly the same taxes as workers without these relations. A two-earner couple may pay twice the taxes of a single-earner couple, but receive only one-third more in benefits.[6]

[6]For further discussion of these inequities, see Peter J. Ferrara, *Social Security: The Inherent Contradiction* (Washington: Cato Institute, 1980), chap. 6.

One of the most blatant social security inequities is that many workers must pay for the program's survivors insurance even though they are not eligible for survivors benefits. This includes single workers without children and many childless two-earner couples. Married workers without children are not eligible for survivors benefits until retirement. Through Super IRAs, these workers could substitute private life insurance for social security survivors insurance and receive all the benefits they pay for. Workers with little or no dependent obligations who might not need or desire such insurance coverage could instead devote some or all of the funds for such insurance to their own retirement.

Other major inequities in social security's current benefit structure bear particularly harshly on blacks and other minorities. The life expectancy of blacks is significantly less than that of whites, and consequently blacks can expect to live fewer years in retirement to collect social security benefits. Blacks, therefore, will receive less benefits than whites due to this factor, though they are subject to the same taxes throughout their working careers. A black male born today has a life expectancy of 64.9 years, two years less than the normal retirement age of 67 that will apply to him.[7] Overall, this black male can expect 50 percent less in retirement benefits than a white male born today due to the difference in life expectancies. In addition, blacks are, on the whole, significantly younger than whites, and since the program offers a worse deal the younger one is, the program discriminates against blacks on this account as well. Other minority groups, such as Hispanics, also have lower-than-average life expectancies, or younger-than-average populations, and consequently also suffer these inequities.

Through Super IRAs, blacks and other minorities could be allowed to pool their saved assets in joint funds that would pay monthly annuity benefits based on the lower life expectancies of these groups. This would result in higher monthly benefits for minority group members. Alternatively, a black or other minority worker could choose to live off the principal and interest of his own Super-IRA funds at his own conservatively set pace, and leave any remaining funds at death to his children or other heirs. For most of today's young workers, the interest on their Super-IRA funds alone would likely be higher than promised social security benefits, making it

[7]National Center for Policy Analysis, *The Effect of the Social Security System on Black Americans* (Dallas, 1983).

easy to maintain self-support without an annuity. In addition, the younger workers who comprise relatively more of the black and other minority populations would gain the most from the higher Super-IRA returns, since social security offers them the worst deal now.

The proposed Super-IRA reform would also strengthen the economy. Based on the initial reform package alone, workers paying into Super IRAs could potentially increase national savings by tens of billions of dollars each year. This in turn would provide the capital necessary for technological innovation, the creation of new jobs, and more rapid economic growth. With a maximally expanded, complete Super-IRA option, annual private savings could potentially be almost doubled, with hundreds of billions of dollars in increased savings possibly flowing into the capital markets annually. Such a savings increase could eventually increase GNP by almost 20 percent.[8] Eventual possible payroll tax reductions would also stimulate job creation and economic growth.

The poor would be particularly helped by the Super-IRA reform. Lower-income workers typically leave school and start work at an earlier age than workers with higher incomes, yet social security credits workers with little, if any, additional benefits for such early years of work and tax payments. Through Super IRAs, however, these workers would receive greater-than-average benefits for such early contributions, since the funds would have more years to accumulate interest before retirement. Moreover, single workers are much more likely to be poor than are married couples, yet social security pays additional benefits to married workers that are not available to single workers, though all are taxed at the same levels. Married and single workers would receive the same market returns through Super IRAs.[9]

The higher retirement benefits available through Super IRAs would be most valuable to the poor, enabling them to buy more of the basic necessities. Similarly, the beneficial economic impact of the reform would open up new opportunities most vitally needed by the poor. Any eventual reductions in the regressive payroll tax

[8]See Martin Feldstein, "Social Insurance," Harvard Institute of Economic Research Discussion Paper no. 477 (Cambridge, Mass., May 1976): 33.

[9]For further discussion of social security's discriminatory impacts on the poor, see Ferrara, *The Inherent Contradiction*, chap. 6.

would also benefit the poor the most, since the tax falls most harshly on those with lower incomes.

Moreover, the reform would create special new opportunities for the poor because it would give them control over some capital through their Super IRAs. As indicated in chapter 1, if a career minimum-wage earner entering the work force today could pay into a Super IRA, along with his employer, the same amounts that would be required by social security, then at market returns he would accumulate almost $300,000 in today's dollars by retirement. This fund could pay him out of interest alone more than he is currently promised under social security and could be left intact to serve as a sturdy foundation for his children.

The supplemental security income (SSI) program would continue to provide means-tested, general revenue–financed welfare benefits to the elderly poor, ensuring that their retirement income would not in any event fall below a basic minimum. Moreover, Super IRAs would allow for greater reliance on this program and for the reduction or elimination of the current waste resulting from the payment of welfare benefits through social security. A substantial portion of social security benefits is based on a welfare, rather than insurance, rationale: payment of these benefits is not based on past taxes paid into the program, but on certain criteria thought to indicate that the beneficiary might be in need. But since social security benefits are paid without a means test to limit such benefits to those actually in need, this welfare assistance ends up going to too many who are not in need.[10] Super IRAs, however, would provide no such backdoor welfare benefits, paying only what workers have earned through past payments into the system. Consequently, the more workers opted for Super IRAs over social security, the more the payment of welfare benefits would be limited to the means-tested SSI program, which pays benefits only to those who are actually in need, and therefore the more the current waste of welfare benefits paid through social security would be eliminated.

In addition, the more workers across the whole economy were allowed to accumulate substantial assets in Super IRAs, the more equal the national distribution of wealth would become. If all workers paid into Super IRAs rather than social security, the national

[10]For further discussion of this problem, see ibid.

concentration of wealth would be reduced by one-third.[11] Yet this would be achieved not by redistributing existing wealth, but by providing an opportunity for the creation of new wealth more equally distributed. Through Super-IRA investments each worker would be developing a substantial ownership stake in America's business and industry. This would revolutionize political attitudes, for instead of retirees tending to develop a psychology of dependence on and support for big government, as is the case with social security, they would tend to support private enterprise and free markets.

Structurally, the reform would "denationalize" the large portion of the pension and insurance industries now represented by social security, shifting functions to the private sector that could be better performed there. It is particularly ridiculous that simple and easily available private life insurance coverage is being displaced by social security survivors benefits. The proposed initial reform package would address this absurdity from the start.

Finally, as the reform reduced social security expenditures through reliance on Super IRAs, federal spending would be substantially reduced. Social security today accounts for about 30 percent of all federal spending. With a complete option to rely on maximally expanded Super IRAs, all of this spending could potentially be taken out of the federal budget altogether and shifted to the private sector. There might be some relatively slight increase in SSI spending as that program picked up the welfare functions of social security, but on net if almost all workers eventually opted for Super IRAs, federal spending would probably be decreased by more than one-fourth. No other reform offers the potential for such a massive reduction in federal spending, not only without hurting anyone, but indeed probably making virtually everyone better off at the same time. With social security, national defense, and interest on the national debt accounting for almost 70 percent of federal spending, it is hard to imagine any major reduction in federal spending without such reform.

The combined benefits of the reform seem quite simply awesome and overwhelming. Few legislative acts could do so much to increase the liberty and prosperity of the American people.

---

[11]Martin Feldstein, "Social Security and the Distribution of Wealth," *Journal of the American Statistical Association* (December 1976).

Variations on a Theme

The above-proposed reform package is based primarily on allowing all workers to substitute Super IRAs for a certain percentage of social security to start, and expanding that percentage over time. This "Percentage Increment" approach has the advantage of involving and, therefore, appealing to all workers from the start.[12] It also allows the government relatively strong control over the amount of income tax revenue it loses over time as a result of the reform. But there are other possible approaches to phasing in the Super-IRA option as well.

The "Younger Workers" Alternative

One alternative would be to allow a full Super-IRA option initially only for workers under a certain age. For example, the reform could be structured exactly as above, except that it would apply only to workers under 30, and these workers would be allowed the option of substituting Super IRAs for social security as much as they wanted. These workers would be allowed to contribute to their IRAs each year an amount up to 100 percent of their employee social security taxes, in addition to other amounts they may currently contribute, with a full dollar-for-dollar income tax credit for such contributions. Workers could also direct their employers to match such contributions, with the employers receiving full compensating income tax credits as well. Workers would then have their future social security benefits reduced to the extent that they took advantage of this option over their careers, with the superior Super-IRA benefits in replacement. Certain portions of the full tax credit would be contingent on workers' purchasing appropriate amounts of life, disability, and retirement health insurance with the funds in their Super IRAs. These options would continue to be available to workers originally under 30 as they grew older as well as to all new young workers, and consequently such options would eventually apply to the entire work force.

The income tax revenue loss in the first year under this approach would be roughly twice as large as that for the income tax credit with the cap of 20 percent of OASI taxes in the reform package proposed above. Moreover, as workers initially under 30 grew

---

[12]Because future social security benefits would be reduced less for those taking the Super-IRA tax credits the older a worker is, as discussed above, the option is structured to make it worthwhile for workers of all ages.

older, the income tax revenue loss would tend to grow because more and more workers would be eligible for the credits each year. The Super-IRA investments would produce new tax revenues that would eventually stabilize the net revenue loss and then start reducing it. Social security expenditure reductions to offset the revenue loss would not start until workers initially under 30 began to retire, but once these workers did so the remaining net revenue loss would be quite rapidly offset due to such expenditure reductions, as the new retirees would largely be relying on Super IRAs rather than social security. The initial revenue losses could be lowered by lowering the initial age of eligibility, perhaps even restricting the applicability of the option only to new workers. But the long-term pattern of net revenue loss would still be the same.

The chief problem with this approach as compared with the Percentage Increment approach in the reform package proposed above is that the net revenue loss would be less controllable. Once such reform were established, the net revenue loss would grow inexorably over several years, and the government would have to be prepared to accommodate it. Under the Percentage Increment approach above, expansions of the Super-IRA option could be adopted by new legislation when the government became fiscally capable of absorbing the new revenue losses, perhaps not until after the revenue loss from prior steps had been largely offset, if necessary. Another problem would be the setting of the cutoff age for when the options would initially apply. Workers above that age would never have the opportunity for a Super-IRA option and might object to the special treatment given those below that age. In any event, they would have little interest in supporting the reform.

An advantage of this approach is that it would set in motion an inevitable movement toward the complete option to substitute Super IRAs for all of social security, which should be the ultimate goal. Under the Percentage Increment approach, new legislative action would be necessary for expansion to a complete option, unless an automatic schedule of expansion were legislatively established from the beginning. It should be noted, however, that under the Younger Workers alternative it would take decades for the full option to be phased in, and it may be possible to reach this point more rapidly through other approaches. Another advantage of the Younger Workers approach is that it would focus reform on those now suffering the worst deal under social security.

The "Older Workers" Alternative

Another alternative would be to allow the full Super-IRA option initially only for workers over a certain age. For example, the reform could be structured exactly as under the Younger Workers alternative above, except that it would initially apply only to workers over 50 rather than workers under 30. The reduction in future social security benefits for those who chose the Super-IRA option would still leave these workers with higher overall benefits.[13] Later legislative acts could provide for the option to apply to increasingly younger workers until it eventually applied to the entire work force.

The initial net revenue loss under this approach would be about the same as that under the Younger Workers alternative above. But there would be no tendency for the net revenue loss to increase over time. Rather, the net loss would tend to decrease rapidly as these older workers retired and began to reduce social security expenditures due to their greater reliance on Super IRAs rather than social security.

The net revenue loss would clearly be more controllable and more easily manageable under this Older Workers alternative as compared with the Younger Workers alternative. Increases in the net loss would result only from express legislative action expanding the Super-IRA option to include younger workers, and the revenue loss would be offset more quickly by expenditure reductions than under any other possible approach. While the setting of the cutoff age for initial eligibility would still be a problem, at least all workers could look forward to some years with the Super-IRA option.

Moreover, older workers would likely be the most sophisticated with respect to the investment possibilities available through Super IRAs and the most eager to take advantage of them. These workers, closest to retirement, would also likely be the ones most worried about the changes in social security, and focusing the Super-IRA option on them first might offset such fears.

However, this approach does not address the most serious problems, which are faced by young workers, except through some relief later in their careers. It may lag in political appeal because it limits the Super-IRA option initially to only a certain age group.

[13]This would result under the same benefit reduction formula as described for the other alternatives above, since the reductions would be less for older workers due to the fewer years remaining before retirement for their Super-IRA contributions to earn and accumulate returns.

208

The "Benefit Type" Alternative

Still another alternative would be to initially allow all workers to substitute Super IRAs entirely for just one type of benefits under social security, and then expand the option to other types over time. For example, at the start workers could simply be allowed to substitute life insurance purchased through their IRAs for social security survivors insurance, exactly as under the second income tax credit in the reform package proposed above.[14] As a later step, workers could be allowed in the same way to substitute private disability insurance purchased through their IRAs for social security disability insurance. That is, workers could be allowed to contribute additional amounts to their IRAs up to the amount of the disability portion of their social security taxes (DI), with matching amounts from their employers, for the purchase of private disability insurance, with full 100 percent income tax credits to both employer and employee for these contributions. Workers would then have any future social security benefits reduced to the extent that they utilized this credit to purchase private disability insurance in effect when they became disabled.

A later expansion would allow workers to set aside additional funds in their IRAs up to the amount of the hospital insurance portion of their social security taxes (HI), with matching amounts from their employers, for the purchase of private health insurance in retirement to replace social security's health insurance, with employer and employee receiving 100 percent income tax credits for these contributions. Finally, workers could be allowed to contribute additional amounts to their IRAs up to the remaining portion of their social security taxes, with matching amounts from their employers, to finance workers' retirement benefits, with full 100 percent income tax credits for employer and employee. Workers would then have their future social security retirement benefits reduced to the extent that they utilized this option over their careers. This option would operate just as the first income tax credit in the reform package proposed above,[15] except that the option here would apply to all retirement benefits, while the credit in the other package would apply only to a fraction of such benefits. Of course, the options for these different types of benefits could be adopted in a different order.

[14]See pp. 196–97.
[15]See pp. 194–95.

209

The survivors insurance option would involve a low initial revenue loss, rapidly offset by resulting reduced social security expenditures, as discussed in regard to the reform package proposed earlier. Private life insurance is also the most simple and most easily understood of all the private alternatives to social security, and it is already routinely utilized by most of the population. Consequently, starting the reform here might be especially attractive practically and politically. Under this Benefit-Type approach, the net revenue loss would remain controllable as the complete Super-IRA option was phased in.

The "Job Related" Alternative

Still another approach would be to allow a full Super-IRA option, as described under the Younger Workers alternative, first to workers in certain industries, and then eventually expand the option industry by industry until it applied to the entire work force. For example, the option could apply first to all union workers. Unions could then assist these workers in taking greatest advantage of the option, perhaps setting up voluntary pools for investment and insurance purchases. Workers would still be able to choose individually whether or how much to substitute Super IRAs for their social security coverage. The option could be expanded next to all government employees, then to all self-employed workers, then to all professional workers, then to nonunion employees of all large manufacturing companies, then perhaps finally to all workers.

The advantage of this approach is that the Super-IRA option could be focused first on those workers who might have the greatest interest in such an option and who might have the most assistance or ability in first utilizing it. Unions, for example, should be quite interested in helping their workers tailor their own systems of retirement and insurance coverage to suit their needs and preferences. The keen interest of government workers in alternatives to social security has long been demonstrated, with their years of heavy lobbying for continued exemption from the program, recently undercut by the 1983 legislation to save social security from bankruptcy. Self-employed and professional workers would also likely have a special interest in such an option because of their likely knowledge of and facility with the opportunities that would be available through Super IRAs. As these workers demonstrated the success and feasibility of the Super-IRA option, it could be extended to other workers. This approach is analogous to the system in Great Britain discussed in chapter 6.

There are several problems with the Job-Related alternative in the context of the United States and the Super IRA. Administrative difficulties would arise if individual workers moved from employment in industries where the option applied to industries where the option did not yet apply, though these difficulties could possibly be addressed by allowing workers to continue to be covered by the option once they worked in jobs where it did apply. Administrative difficulties might also arise in defining the industrial groups to which the option should apply and those to which it should not. Finally, workers initially excluded from the option for no apparently necessary reason might object too strongly for this approach to be feasible. Still, it is a theoretically possible alternative approach.

The "Smorgasbord" Alternative

A final alternative would be to mix any of the above alternatives in a legislative package. For example, younger workers alone could be allowed the Super-IRA option and for only a certain percentage of their social security retirement coverage. Or younger workers could be allowed an option first only for survivors insurance. Many such combinations would be possible.

Income Tax Credits vs. Payroll Tax Credits

Each of the above alternative reform approaches is based on allowing workers the option of taking a credit against income taxes for extra IRA contributions. This has the advantage of not reducing payroll taxes flowing into social security to pay benefits for today's elderly, in fact strengthening social security over the long run as the reform reduces expenditures while maintaining revenues.

Alternatively, each of the above reform approaches could be based instead on allowing workers a credit against social security payroll taxes rather than income taxes. In other respects the above reform alternatives would each remain the same. The payroll tax credit may be more desirable when social security has a large trust fund accumulation, like that now projected to begin in the 1990s under the SSA's intermediate assumptions. If options based on income tax credits were initially adopted, it might be necessary to base later, expansionary options on payroll tax credits. This is because the earlier income tax credit options could produce unwieldy social security surpluses as expenditures were reduced through greater reliance on IRAs but payroll taxes were maintained. The later payroll tax credits would absorb such surpluses.

The payroll tax credit alternative means losing the feature of strengthening social security financing that is offered by approaches based on an income tax credit. It also means facing charges, however illegitimate, of "weakening social security," since the program itself would lose some revenue from payroll tax credits. But if social security has sufficiently large surpluses when the reform is proposed, these drawbacks should not be important.

Perhaps the best way to advance a payroll tax credit option is as a contingency. The proposal could provide that as social security trust funds rose above a certain surplus level, say, 150 percent of one year's expenditures, then a modest payroll tax credit option could be triggered equal to, say, 10 percent of OASI taxes for each worker and his employer. This would assure the public that the option would not undermine social security financing.

Other Surplus Contingencies

Since current rapid economic growth is creating the possibility of substantial annual social security surpluses (as discussed in the *Comment* following chapter 2), other provisions contingent on the development of such surpluses could be included in the reform package. For example, legislation could provide that when social security trust funds reached 150 percent of one year's expenditures, a portion of the payroll tax increases now scheduled for 1988 and 1990 would be repealed. A return to the threshold level of 150 percent would result in the repeal of another portion of these tax increases, and so on until they were entirely repealed.

This payroll tax rollback would only heighten the need for long-term reform based on Super IRAs. As we saw in chapter 2, social security is currently relying on the development of substantial surpluses from 1990 to 2020 to pay benefits to the baby-boom generation and today's young workers. Eliminating the 1988 and 1990 tax increases, however, would sharply reduce or eliminate altogether any major trust fund accumulation over this period, leaving inadequate financial support for the benefits of the baby boomers and others after 2020. However, if we adopted sufficient Super-IRA options now, this long-term problem would be avoided as well. Post-2020 retirees would be relying less on social security and much more on Super IRAs, reducing social security expenditures sharply and consequently eliminating the financial gap.

212

Another alternative contingency provision could address any short-term financial problem in the HI portion of social security. Despite recent improvement in the short-term outlook, HI is expected to run short of funds before the end of the next decade, as we saw in the *Comment* after chapter 2. A fundamental reform package could provide, however, that any surplus in the rest of social security (OASDI) could be used to fund HI. This would allow the social security program as a whole to continue paying benefits until Super IRAs permanently solved any remaining financial problems. A big advantage of this provision is that it would avoid any short-term HI collapse without a further payroll tax increase to bail it out. Otherwise, it is extremely unlikely that any such short-term problem would be solved entirely, or frankly even primarily, by benefit cuts, leading to further large payroll tax increases.

Conclusion

The reform package described in detail earlier[16] is offered as one feasible and politically attractive approach. But different legislators may have different perspectives that may lead them to favor an alternative approach. Consequently, a broad range of different possible approaches has been discussed here so that alternative legislative packages can be designed if thought desirable.

Conventional Reform Approaches

What are the alternatives to the above-described Super-IRA reform approaches?

For conservatives, the knee-jerk response is still to attempt to solve the problems of social security by cutting benefits substantially. But in return for the obvious, high political costs of pursuing such an approach, the achievements attained, if any, are likely to be only marginal. One can imagine only the tiniest benefit cuts ever being politically feasible in the short run for those already retired. Perhaps more significant benefit reductions might be politically feasible over the long run for retirees in the future, under legislation enacted now, far in advance, though frankly even this would be highly questionable. But far greater expenditure reductions over the long run could be made painlessly by inducing workers now to provide for their retirement through Super IRAs and the private sector instead. The benefit-cut game is clearly just not worth the candle when an alternative approach is available—Super IRAs—

[16]See pp. 194–97.

that would accomplish the same results and more, without the high political costs and, indeed, potentially with great political advantages rather than costs.

In the abstract, Super IRAs may somehow appear more radical than just cutting benefits. But in the concrete, to the average worker, the freedom to substitute Super IRAs for social security and consequently receive higher benefits in the future, while benefits for presently retired relatives were maintained, should seem far less radical than significant unexpected cuts for retired relatives today and a simple repudiation of a large portion of the worker's own promised benefits in the future. Real people don't live in the abstract.

Moreover, simple spending reductions would not solve all the problems of the program. Even with such cuts, we would ultimately have the same huge government program with the same problems, although on a marginally smaller scale. If the benefit reductions did no more than create a balance between revenues and expenditures in a pay-as-you-go system, the program would even still be subject to periodic financial crises. Indeed, substantial benefit cuts would make at least one key problem worse. Since significant cuts are unlikely to be made for those already retired, the vast majority of any large-scale benefit reductions would likely fall on the future benefits promised to today's young workers. Yet it is these workers who are already promised inadequate, below-market returns under social security, in contrast to the high, above-market returns paid to today's retirees. Such cuts would consequently only exacerbate this intergenerational inequity and make the intolerably low returns offered to today's young people even lower.

Another reform approach advanced in conservative circles is to overhaul the social security benefit structure so that workers would receive in benefits precisely what they paid in taxes at some imputed interest rate and on an actuarial basis. Total social security spending would be the same, but the benefit distribution would be sharply altered.

Such reform would yield some important benefits,[17] but its advocates have not fully appreciated the again harsh, probably prohibitive, political costs it would entail. These would arise because any

[17]Such a reform would enhance economic efficiency and eliminate many, but not all, of the program's inequities as well as reduce the waste of welfare benefits through the current system. See Ferrara, *The Inherent Contradiction*, chaps. 3 and 6.

214

such overhaul of the program's benefit structure would result in substantial losses of social security benefits for a large portion of the population while another portion gained through redistribution. The large number of losers could naturally be expected to block such reform. Moreover, the redistributions involved here would be especially unattractive politically because benefits would be shifted from lower- and lower-middle-income workers to higher-middle-income workers. Benefits would also be shifted heavily from traditional families to single and/or childless and/or two-earner-couple workers just at a time when the political clout of the traditional family has grown, particularly as a base for the conservative politicians who might be most expected to advance such reform.

Moreover, once again, the goal of such reform—a rationalized benefit structure—would be achieved more easily through Super IRAs because benefits through these accounts would be paid on precisely such a rationalized basis. That is, benefits would be equal to contributions paid in, plus interest, on an actuarial basis. But Super IRAs would not have the same political costs as simple social security–benefit restructuring because they would offer higher benefits in the future to all groups of young workers today, as indicated in chapter 1. Those favored by the current social security structure would receive somewhat less of an increase in benefits than would the currently disfavored, but they would still receive a huge increase. Such relative differences in improvement simply would not arouse significant opposition, unlike a situation of major wins and losses, especially since the improvement would swamp the differences, the differences would result from the elimination of widely perceived inequities in the current system, and the relatively less favored traditionalists would predominantly support Super-IRA reform on general conservative principles anyway.

In addition, simple social security–benefit restructuring would again not solve all the major problems and offer all the major advantages that Super IRAs would. In particular, it would still leave today's younger workers with inadequate, below-market returns from the program. It would also maintain the current high level of government spending for social security. Consequently, such restructuring alone would just not be worth the political costs when the same goal could be achieved through the far more beneficial and politically advantageous alternative of Super IRAs.

Unfortunately, some of the most ardent proponents of benefit-restructuring advance most passionately not their own proposed reforms, but the proposition that no reform shifting to greater reliance on the private sector is politically feasible. So convinced of this are they that they will actually join a fight to the bitter end to prevent such reform, presumably to prove their point. These proponents are consequently part of the problem rather than the solution. Simple benefit restructuring alone can never be acceptable to conservatives committed to expanding the role of private markets and reducing the role of government.

As suggested in the introduction, the thinking of liberals regarding social security reform has been dominated by the program's establishment old guard, which refuses to consider any major changes in the program except further tax increases. This anachronistic old guard notwithstanding, social security taxes have reached a level where increasing them further would involve prohibitive political costs as well. Moreover, raising taxes would not solve any of the program's problems and would make many worse. Benefits for today's young workers would represent an even lower return on the higher taxes. The economy would be further damaged. If the higher taxes did no more than create a balance between revenues and expenditures in a pay-as-you-go system, the program would still be subject to periodic financial crises. Indeed, higher taxes themselves could contribute to future financial crises by weakening the economy.

Fortunately, some liberals have begun to dissent from the old guard. Some have been heard to question the impact of the payroll tax on the economy and whether young workers can continue to afford further tax increases. Some have noticed the impact of the program on the federal budget, squeezing out programs targeted for the poor. Some have shown heightened sensitivity to the inequities of the program. These liberals of the future have not developed a coherent strategy for reform, but at least they are starting to ask fundamental questions about a very questionable status quo.

The conventional approaches to social security's problems are inadequate, and they are unacceptable to the American people. Super IRAs offer an effective reform alternative that should be quite attractive to both conservatives and liberals, and to the broad public at large, as discussed below.

The Prospects for Real Reform

In chapter 5, we examined changes relating to social security that are sharply improving the prospects for real, fundamental reform of the program. These changes result from the maturing of social security's pay-as-you-go system. When such a system is begun there are no accrued benefit obligations, and the funds flowing into the pay-as-you-go system can be immediately paid out. This means that early beneficiaries get free windfall benefits they did not pay for and receive high returns on whatever they did pay, while the system appears to be running huge surpluses and faces no threat of bankruptcy. This explains the past popularity of the program.

But once the first working generation that has paid full taxes into such a system throughout all working years retires, the picture changes dramatically. Now there are huge benefit obligations accrued with no reserves saved to back them up. It is no longer possible to pay out free windfall benefits. Instead, the system faces periodic threats of bankruptcy, and unexpected tax increases and benefit cuts are necessary to save it. The huge tax burdens placed on workers to finance accrued benefit obligations mean that even if all the program's promised benefits are paid to these workers, such benefits would still represent a low, below-market return on past tax payments. These developments naturally produce a major, unfavorable shift in public opinion regarding the program.

The U.S. social security system is now entering its mature phase, and these problems are all now appearing. Public attitudes toward the program are becoming less favorable, creating the opportunity for fundamental reform. These problems can only worsen in the future, and public opinion regarding the program will consequently turn more unfavorable, steadily producing an increasingly receptive climate for reform.

To complete this picture, we will examine here key factors relating to the proposed Super-IRA reform package that further enhance the prospects for real reform. The most fundamental of these are the extraordinary benefits of such reform, which we have already discussed. Naturally, any reform offering such great benefits has bright prospects for eventual adoption.

But probably equally important is the manner in which the reform proposes to attain these advantages. The social security benefits of the elderly would not be cut in any way. Instead, the elderly would be guaranteed that once they retired, Congress would be constitutionally obligated to pay them all their promised benefits. The reform would also sharply strengthen social security's financial ability to pay its promised benefits, further improving the security of the elderly. Moreover, today's workers would not be required to

217

participate in the Super-IRA option if they did not desire to do so. Workers also could forgo this option completely and remain entirely in social security as is, without change.

Structured in this way, the reform would not take anything away from anybody. It would simply increase the freedom and options of workers. There is consequently no reason why the reform should be anything but enormously popular.

Our proposed initial reform package would itself allow workers to substitute Super IRAs only for at most one-fifth of their social security retirement benefits and for pre-age-65 social security survivors insurance. Workers would still in any event retain 80 percent of their social security retirement benefits. Why shouldn't workers who believe they can get a better deal in the private sector through Super IRAs be allowed at least this limited opportunity to do so? With benefits for the elderly guaranteed, and social security itself strengthened at the same time, this question should become politically unanswerable.

The proposed reform should naturally appeal to the elderly because of the great care taken to guarantee their benefits and improve the financial strength of social security. But the reform should have even more appeal to those who hold the key to the political future, today's young workers, particularly the politically aware and active young urban professionals, or "yuppies." Among many other benefits, the reform would grant young workers across the board the opportunity for higher retirement benefits, an end to the great financial doubts and uncertainties about their future produced by social security, and the opportunity to work in a more healthy and growing economy now. Young professionals will most readily understand these advantages of the reform. Moreover, because of the higher-than-average incomes of the yuppies and the prevalence of single workers and two-earner couples among them, they receive especially low returns from social security. They would consequently especially benefit from the higher returns offered by Super IRAs. They would also particularly benefit from the ability to avoid social security survivors insurance through the reform, since single, childless, and two-earner-couple workers generally receive little or no benefit from such insurance.

The Super-IRA reform also offers both liberals and conservatives important reasons to support it. For liberals, the reform would improve the security of the elderly and provide increased freedom and flexibility for today's workers. It would reduce or eliminate inequities and discrimination negatively affecting the poor, minorities, and working women. It would provide increased benefits and improved economic opportunties especially important to the poor. It would produce a more equal distribution of wealth and could eventually lead to sharp reductions in the regressive payroll tax.

For conservatives, the reform would potentially produce a major reduction in the size and scope of government, with steep reductions in taxes and spending. It would increase reliance on the private sector, free markets, and individual responsibility and control. It would expand economic freedom and improve economic efficiency. It would base benefit payments on what has been earned and paid for, rather than on welfare criteria.

A special problem for the reform is created by the currently large federal budget deficits. These deficits will arouse special resistance to the income tax revenue loss produced by the reform over the short run, since the loss would temporarily increase already unusually large deficits in the next few years. However, the reform has been carefully designed to avoid a large loss of income tax revenues at any one time. In normal circumstances, the initial loss of around $15 billion in revenues annually in the context of trillion-dollar budgets would not be an insurmountable political barrier as long as the benefits were worth the cost, as they seem to be here by a wide margin.

Today's special circumstances of unusually large federal deficits should not prevent the reform's adoption. The reform and its benefits are extremely important and are needed now, and the magnitude of the revenue loss is still manageable. Moreover and most importantly, the reform itself, as we have noted, would produce new savings through the Super IRAs that should at least offset any increase in government borrowing resulting from the revenue loss. Consequently, there would be no net increase in the government borrowing drain on private savings, the major concern behind worry over increased budget deficits. Given this, it would be ironic and misguided to allow concern over budget deficits today to prevent adoption of a reform that would probably reduce federal spending sharply over the long run.

In any event, if politically necessary, the reform could be phased in more gradually or start more slowly. The effective date of the first Super-IRA income tax credit of our proposed reform package, relating to retirement benefits, could be delayed until January 1, 1988. For FY 1988, therefore, the credit would apply only to three-fourths of the fiscal year, further reducing the loss for that year. Or the reform could start instead with the low-cost survivors insurance option first, the second income tax credit in our proposed package. Eventually, the special budget-deficit problem of today will be resolved one way or another and will no longer pose a significant difficulty for the reform.

The only remaining element necessary for adoption of the reform is leadership. Innovative leadership is needed to recognize that Super IRAs offer a true and honest solution to currently intractable problems. Articulate leadership is needed to express the value of the reform effectively. Timely leadership is needed, as the problems of social security must be addressed now, not after the next crisis is upon us.

Perhaps those in leadership positions today are too enthralled by Big Government ideology, or too comfortable and cozy with the Washington bureaucratic establishment, or too unimaginative and dispirited to recognize the need and opportunity for real social security reform as offered by the Super-IRA option. If so, these inadequacies will delay such reform. But they will not stop it. Rather, our society, as it has done so often in the past, will call forth new leaders with the vision and spirit to meet the demands and needs of the times. And with such new leadership, the prospects for real reform will look very good indeed.

About the Editor

Peter J. Ferrara is a Washington attorney and chairman of the advisory committee of the Independent Retirement Alliance. He previously served as a senior staff member in the White House Office of Policy Development and as special assistant to the assistant secretary for policy development at the Department of Housing and Urban Development. An adjunct scholar of the Cato Institute, he is the author of *Social Security: The Inherent Contradiction* and *Social Security: Averting the Crisis*.

Cato Institute

Founded in 1977, the Cato Institute is a public policy research foundation dedicated to broadening the parameters of policy debate to allow consideration of more options that are consistent with the traditional American principles of limited government, individual liberty, and peace. Toward that goal, the Institute strives to achieve a greater involvement of the intelligent, concerned lay public in questions of policy and the proper role of government.

The Institute is named for *Cato's Letters*, pamphlets that were widely read in the American Colonies in the early eighteenth century and played a major role in laying the philosophical foundation for the revolution that followed. Since that revolution, civil and economic liberties have been eroded as the number and complexity of social problems have grown. Today virtually no aspect of human life is free from the domination of a governing class of politico-economic interests. A pervasive intolerance for individual rights is shown by government's arbitrary intrusions into private economic transactions and its disregard for civil liberties.

To counter this trend the Cato Institute undertakes an extensive publications program dealing with the complete spectrum of policy issues. Books, monographs, and shorter studies are commissioned to examine the federal budget, social security, regulation, NATO, international trade, and a myriad of other issues. Major policy conferences are held throughout the year from which papers are published thrice yearly in the *Cato Journal*. The Institute maintains an informal joint publishing arrangement with the Johns Hopkins University Press.

In order to maintain an independent posture, the Cato Institute accepts no government funding. Contributions are received from foundations, corporations, and individuals, and other revenue is generated from the sale of publications. The Institute is a non-profit, tax-exempt, educational foundation under Section 501(c)3 of the Internal Revenue Code.

CATO INSTITUTE
224 Second St., S.E.
Washington, D.C. 20003